Pure Land Haiku:
The Art of Priest Issa

D1453585

David G. Lanoue

HaikuGuy.com
New Orleans, Louisiana, USA

ISBN-10: 0-9912840-4-6
ISBN-13: 978-0-9912840-4-7

First edition published in 2004 by Buddhist
Books International
820 Plumas St.
Reno, Nevada 89509

Electronic Edition 2013 by the author
HaikuGuy.com

Pure Land Haiku:
The Art of Priest Issa

for Kathleen, who showed me how

and for Dr. Matsunaga, who made it possible

TABLE OF CONTENTS

ACKNOWLEDGEMENTS

I thank Robin D.Gill, who generously helped with the translations; Hiroshi Kobori, who provided insights on some particularly difficult haiku; and Shinji Ōgawa, who did both. Much of this book was written in 1999 as my sabbatical project at Xavier University of Louisiana; I am grateful to the committee of my peers who recommended me and the administrators who approved me. My mentor at the University of Nebraska-Lincoln, Paul A. Olson, has always been a guiding presence; though his work is in English literature, he set me on a path that led me to Japan and Issa; in my criticism I attempt to apply the same sensible, semantic approach as he has done in Chaucer studies. And to Bob Spiess, who published parts of this evolving work over the years in *Modern Haiku* magazine, and who, from the very beginning, encouraged me in my research; my deepest thanks. He is gone but never forgotten.

Preface to the Second Edition

In 2004 Dr. Daigan Lee Matsunaga of Buddhist Books International took a chance and published the first edition of this study. I met him in the flesh in Tokyo in October of 2007, when he invited me to give a lecture on Issa and Pure Land Buddhism at Higashi Honganji temple. Even during our first interview in a sitting room of the temple, sipping green tea, we discussed the possibility of one day bringing out a revised edition. Unfortunately, his subsequent health problems put that dream on hold, and then, sadly, this great, wise, and generous scholar passed away. I dedicated the first edition of this work to my partner, Kathleen E. Davis; I dedicate this second edition to Kathleen and to Dr. Matsunaga. As I prepared the original manuscript, Kathleen was working on her own book, an exploration of Blanca Valmont's fashion writing. We wrote together, often in our favorite New Orleans coffee shop at the time, and she gave me sharp and invaluable advice on how to gather my seemingly random observations into an organized argument. She "showed me how." And Dr. Matsunaga, by agreeing to publish this labor of so many years, made it possible for my insights about Issa to reach a wide audience. I am eternally grateful to her and to him.

INTRODUCTION. *ICHI DAIJI:*
The One Great Thing

As a one-breath burst of language, a haiku must say everything it needs to say in that one breath. A haiku is immediate and experiential.

> おれとして白眼くらする蛙かな
> *ore to shite niramekura suru kawazu kana*
> (162.11).[1]

> locked in a staring contest
> me . . .
> and a frog

The above example is typical of the style of Kobayashi Issa (1763-1828)[2], one of Japan's most beloved and prolific poets of haiku. It is succinct yet resonant with meaning. In terms of form, it falls comfortably within mainstream haiku tradition, with seventeen sound units (*onji*) arranged in a 5-7-5 pattern, a season word ("frog" signifying springtime), and a cutting word (*kana*), which functions here as a sort of verbal exclamation point that adds resonance to the whole.[3] Literally, it reads, "With me/ [it] does a staring contest/ a frog!" What makes the poem typical of Issa, so much so that informed readers, seeing it for the first time, will instantly suspect it is his work; are its comic structure and warm acceptance of a small creature as a peer. The image of a grown man crouched to frog level for a staring game is funny in itself, but like a master joke teller Issa initially misdirects our expectation, leading us to suspect that human contestants might be involved. In the punch line, however, we learn that Issa's unblinking opponent is . . . a frog! Explication is hardly needed for one to "get" such a joke. Even a child can do so, effortlessly—and, over the centuries, many have. But herein lies a special challenge to Issa's adult readers. It is tempting to dismiss him as *merely* a child's poet, though to do so would be like reading Dante's *Divine Comedy* as a mere travel adventure, overlooking its allegorical content. Issa's many thousands of one-breath verses, though in a less linear way than Dante's great poem, reveal and explore the cosmology and religious constructs of his culture. While Dante operates within the semantic universe of medieval Christianity, Issa describes a distinctly Japanese Buddhist way of being in, not "of," the world. Though disarmingly simple, his haiku are replete with spiritual meaning and philosophical insight. Children may love him, but a child's poet he is not.

Buddhism provides the subtext for Issa's haiku comedies. His profound, lifelong Buddhist faith encompasses a way of perceiving, conceptualizing, and relating to the universe; his poetry, which is nothing but a record of encounters with that universe, naturally expresses such faith. Returning to our example, we find that the haiku appears in two poetic diaries: *Hachiban nikki* ("Eighth Diary"), of which it is an 1819, Second Month entry[4]; and *Oraga haru* ("My

9

Spring"), also covering the year 1819 but compiled at some later point. In the first manuscript the haiku is prefaced simply with the phrase, "Sitting alone" (4.236), but in *Oraga haru*, a lengthy anecdote about the drowning of an eleven year-old child precedes it, predisposing the reader to view it in a certain light. Issa explains that he attended the child's cremation and was so moved that he composed a *waka*, and old verse form of 31 sound units in a 5-7-5-7-7 arrangement. In it, he compares the boy to fresh, new grass turned to smoke so soon after it had sprouted. He then wonders out loud, "Will not even trees and plants one day become Buddhas?"[5] He answers his own question immediately: "They, too, will acquire Buddha-nature" (6.137). What follows next in the journal is the phrase, "Sitting alone," and the haiku,

> locked in a staring contest
> me . . .
> and a frog.

In the context of *Oraga haru*, then, this humorous verse about a frog and a poet can be viewed as a continuation of Issa's musings on death, loss, and Buddha-nature. Trees will acquire it, grass will acquire it, and even this frog, who, like Issa, sits alone as if rapt in meditation, will realize enlightenment. Issa's frog is an ancient, fellow traveler: a peer on the path to awakening.

He called himself *Issa-bō haikaiji*—Priest Issa (一茶坊) of Haiku Temple (俳諧寺). His priestly way of life, and way of thinking about that life, naturally and profoundly influenced his art.[6] He lived and professed the precepts of Shinran's popular Jōdoshinshū (True Teaching Pure Land) sect but unlike the illiterate masses of its followers reveals a keen understanding of the seminal texts and subtle nuances of Shinran's teaching. Issa's dedicated reader should therefore become familiar with the key ideas of Shinran's school of Buddhism to make sense of his haiku— as the Japanese critics Murata Shōcho and Kaneko Tohta have proposed.[7] Priest Issa's little poems often hinge on specifically Jōdoshinshū concepts of sin, grace, faith, and salvation, as the following example shows.

花桶に蝶も聞かよ一大事
hana oke ni chō mo kiku ka yo ichi daiji
(167.4)

on the flower pot
does the butterfly also hear
Buddha's promise?

The revelatory phrase is the third: *ichi daiji*, which literally denotes, "one great thing." In Jōdoshinshū belief, the "one great thing" that the haiku refers to is the "original vow" (*hongan*: 本願) of Amida Buddha (Sanskrit: Amitābha) to rescue all sentient beings who sincerely invoke his name, insuring their rebirth in his Western Paradise, the Pure Land—a mythic place as well as a metaphor for enlightenment. Here, Issa wonders if the butterfly also hears the good news of salvation, a universal salvation that applies to it as much as it does to the human poet and to his readers. Its stillness implies attentiveness. The butterfly on the flower pot embodies a Pure Land Buddhist ideal: innocent, natural, non-calculating piety.

The French translator, Titus-Carmel, renders the third phrase, "*la Grande Unité*" (31), transforming "one great thing" into "the Great Unity." It is a deft solution to a translation problem, but a vague notion of cosmic unity is not the *precise* focus of the poem. Issa and his butterfly are contemplating a quite specific "great thing": Amida Buddha's promise to enable their rebirth in the Pure Land.

As with our staring frog example, again the diary context helps us probe deeper into Issa's meaning. According to its prescript in the two diaries in which it appears, it was inspired by a memorial service that the poet attended (Kobayashi Issa 2.467; 9.222), suggesting a temple scene wherein the faithful might be chanting the *nembutsu* ("Namu Amida Butsu"), the Pure Land prayer that invokes the name of Amida Buddha in celebration of his saving vow. Or, as R. H. Blyth visualizes it, a priest might be preaching a sermon before an image of Amida (*Haiku* 2.552). Either way, the clearly indicated temple setting with its ritual focus on death and the beyond imbues the delicate, still butterfly with particular religious significance. Once a caterpillar, it not only hears Amida's "One Great Thing" but also palpably stands for the rebirth and transformation that this great thing, this original vow, promises.

The haiku, it turns out, is a revision of an

earlier piece.

あか棚に蝶も聞くかよ一大事
aka tana ni chō mo kikuka yo ichi daiji
(167.4)

on the offering shelf
does the butterfly also hear
Buddha's promise?

In this original version, the butterfly reposes on an offering shelf, a shrine displaying an image of the Buddha along with offerings of water and flowers. In both versions, Issa celebrates simple, trusting faith. Without intent or calculation, the butterfly has landed in the lap of Buddha's mercy. The question, "does the butterfly also hear?" is rhetorical for Issa. Of *course* the butterfly hears Amida Buddha's promise!

Just as some readers and scholars dismiss Issa as a mere child's poet, others, perhaps because of this first perception, question the depth and seriousness of his Buddhism. Among the Japanese, the most notable figure to have held this view is the great Buddhist scholar, D. T. Suzuki. In his book, *Shin Buddhism*, a study of Jōdoshinshū belief, he dismisses Issa as a "worldly" and "spiritually poor" poet whose Buddhism is marred by a whining obsession with his personal lack of money. As evidence of this, Suzuki cites this haiku: "*nanigoto mo/ anata makase no/ toshi no kure*," which he paraphrases: "I, being at the end of the year, having no money whatever to pay my accounts, have no alternative but to let Amida do his will" (62). The haiku in question is the concluding poem of the *Oraga haru*.

ともかくもあなた任せのとしの暮
tomokaku mo anata makase no toshi no kure[8]

come what may
trusting in the Buddha
the year ends

The notion that Issa is throwing up his arms to Amida Buddha for crass financial reasons is not at all supported by the text of the haiku nor by its diary context. Early in that journal he indeed mentions his poverty, describing his "trashy hut" (*kuzu-ya*: 屑家) as a ramshackle structure that, he fears, a strong wind might blow away at any minute (6.136). But in the same passage, he goes on to describe himself as one "covered with the dust of worldliness" (*zokujin ni uzumorete*: 俗塵に埋れて), and so, he concludes, he has no recourse but to trust in the saving power of Amida Buddha (*anata makase*: あなた任せ; 6.135-36). This is exactly the proper attitude that one must cultivate vis-à-vis the "Other Power" of Amida, according to Shinran. There is no reason to suspect that Issa's invocation of the Buddha's grace in this early passage or in the final haiku of the journal—the one cited by Dr. Suzuki—are the laments of a "spiritually poor" individual.

Anyone who has read much of Issa's work soon discovers that his often-mentioned trashy hut stands as a metaphor for the poet himself: a comic, self-deprecating image. With its corners unswept, spiders can rest easy—not only because of the owner's Buddhist compassion but more importantly because, as he repeats often, he would rather do nothing. On New Year's Day, others diligently sweep and decorate their gates with pine-and-bamboo arrangements, but Issa's hermitage remains "just as it is." His detractors take such comic self-irony at face value, viewing the poet as merely lazy, but in doing so they overlook the fact that this attitude of *kono mama*, being "just as I am," is appropriate for the practice of Jōdoshinshū Buddhism. Shinran urges that one not strive or calculate to attain enlightenment but, instead, simply accept Amida Buddha's saving power *kono mama*: just as he or she is, sinful and human.[9]

Refuting Suzuki's dismissal of Issa as a Buddhist is not reason enough for the present book. Issa passed on long ago, so it makes no difference to him whether pundits of later time label him as "spiritually poor" or praise him, as I have done[10], as a consummate Buddhist artist. It is not for his sake but for his readers today that the present study will, I hope, have value. Our understanding of Issa goes deeper when we consider his immense canon of haiku—a lifetime production of over twenty thousand—in light of the Buddhist themes that meant so much to him. These themes include: (1) travel as pilgrimage, (2) human feeling in relation to the bodhisattva ideal, (3) worldly conditions in the Latter Days of Dharma, (4) transience, (5) spontaneity, (6) the doctrine of karma, (7) prayer, and (8) Amida Buddha's grace.

Travel as pilgrimage. Issa refers to himself not only as a priest but as a "Cloud-Water" wanderer (*unsui*: 雲水), claiming his place in a long and revered tradition of itinerant artist-monks. As we will see in Chapter 1, the kind of travel he describes in prose and in haiku is, in conception and practice, a spiritual exercise.

Human feeling, worldly conditions, transience. Though the importance of his Buddhism to his art was forgotten by readers in later, more secular times; those of the pre-Meiji period in which he lived universally appreciated "Priest Issa" in priestly terms. In 1851, twenty-four years after his death, his *Oraga haru* was published. Two postscripts were appended, written by Seian Saiba and Hyōkai Shisanjin. In the first postscript, Seian notes Issa's humor, but declares that "Sarcasm [*hiniku*: 皮肉] is not the main object of this priest . . . his writing also contains loneliness, laughter, and sadness; and it expresses human feeling [*ninjō:*人情], worldly conditions [*setai:* 世態], and transience [*mujō:* 無常]" (6.165). The author of the second postscript, Hyōkai, adds, "Though it has a bit of jest in it, [Issa's poetry] visits well the way of Buddhism . . . boldly not loathing the dust of this world and filled with human feeling [*ninjō:* 人情]" (6.157). In Chapter 2 we will see how Issa's "human feeling" relates to Buddhist compassion and the tradition of the bodhisattva, the enlightened saint who returns to the world of suffering for the sake of others. In Chapter 3, haiku reflections on worldly conditions, particularly the Pure Land Buddhist belief that the present age is depraved and fallen, will be explored. And Issa's treatment of one of

Buddhism's most essential themes, transience, is the topic of Chapter 4.

Sin and spontaneity. Strangely, these concepts are intimately related in Issa's Jōdoshinshū construction of reality. In these depraved, "Latter Days of Dharma," sin is an inevitable part of the human condition. Even those who would escape sin by doing good works and obeying religious precepts, according to Shinran, are doomed to fail. Ego-tainted reliance on "self-power" (*jiriki:* 自力) is not enough. The answer, Shinran proposes and Issa concurs, is to trust absolutely in the saving grace of Amida Buddha, cultivating an attitude of *jinen* (自然): non-striving spontaneity. Without calculation, the devotee emulates Nature's own non-forcing and lets salvation come "of itself"—the literal translation of *jinen* (modern pronunciation = *shizen*). This sin/spontaneity relationship as it plays out in Issa's poetry will be Chapter 5's focus.

Karma. We have already noted that Issa's treatment of nonhuman beings as peers and fellow travelers is a widely recognized hallmark of his style. In his compendious study, *Issa no kenkyū* (1949), Japanese critic Fujimoto Jitsuwa enumerates and provides examples of forty-two aspects of Issa's style, and topping his list, not surprisingly, is "personification" (*gijinhō:* 擬人法), the "human" depiction of animals (415). While Fujimoto correctly stresses personification in Issa, he fails to situate the poet's egalitarian approach to animals and even plants in the context of his Buddhist vision of the universe with its constituent doctrines of reincarnation and karma—our theme for Chapter 6.

Prayer and grace. The related concepts of prayer and the saving power of Amida Buddha definitely deserve examination. Issa, from time to time, lampoons his fellow Buddhists who rattle off the *nembutsu* prayer as if it were a mere incantation to guarantee their rebirth in the Pure Land. Contrary to this popular notion, the chant *Namu Amida Bustsu* ("All Praise to Amida Buddha!") does not ensure salvation—nor is it a request to do so. As we will discover in Chapter 7, it is more accurately understood as a hymn of gratitude for a favor already bestowed. The Other Power (*tariki:* 他力) of Amida Buddha's saving grace provides the guiding principle for Issa's life and haiku.

He was no child's poet, nor was he, as Suzuki claimed, a shallow Buddhist. When we examine his haiku in connection with Pure Land Buddhism, we arrive at a richer and more semantically grounded understanding of what "Priest Issa of Haiku Temple" was about as an artist and as a man.

A Note on Approach

Haiku is not a discursive form of writing. Each little poem records an encounter involving Nature and self without explaining or moralizing. A poet such as Issa does not articulate philosophical arguments or defend religious doctrines in his one-breath verses, and yet philosophical insights and religious beliefs shape his myriad encounters with the universe, recorded over a span of over forty years, 1787 to 1828. Of these many thousands of haiku, no single one encapsulates Issa's vision in totality, so any example chosen to illustrate particular aspects of that vision is arbitrary and could be replaced by dozens, if not hundreds, of others. The important thing is not the uniqueness of a particular poem but the common points that it reveals. The reader should be aware that each haiku cited, while it stands alone as a work of art, echoes many others like it.

A second aspect of my approach has to do with intertextual linkages: relationships of haiku to haiku, of haiku to prose passages in the poet's journals, and of haiku to passages in Buddhist scriptures and commentaries. Such connections could fill many books; for the present one I seek to show those relationships that best reveal the Buddhist themes that run throughout Issa's work: specifically, the topics identified above: pilgrimage, human feeling, the fallen world, transience, sin, spontaneity, karma, prayer, and grace.

Over twenty thousand haiku: an awesome display of creative energy by a master of his chosen form. Of course, we can only probe the tip of such an iceberg in one book, but if our examples are well-chosen and our argument sound, that tip will be a fair representation of the massive structure that looms below.

Chapter 1. *UNSUI:* Cloud-Water Wanderer

The year 1776 was a hard one for Kobayashi Yatarō, the farmer's son who would one day adopt the literary pseudonym of Issa and become known and loved worldwide. By traditional Japanese reckoning, according to which a child is age one at birth and gains a year each New Year's thereafter, that year he turned fourteen. His grandmother died in the eighth lunar month, depriving him of the last vestige of maternal affection in the family home, having lost his mother years before. And then Yatarō grew deathly ill, but luckily for him (and for posterity) his fever eventually broke, and he survived another cold winter in the mountains of Shinano Province, present-day Nagano Prefecture.

The following spring it was time for him to leave snowy Shinano. Years later, in his 1801 *Journal of My Father's Last Days* (*Chichi no shūen nikki:* 父の終焉日記), Issa describes the situation that sent him on the road at such an early age. The speaker in the passage is his dying father, reminiscing.

> Well now, from the time you were three and your mother passed, as you grew older you didn't live in harmony with your new mother. Day after day spirits were injured; night after night flames of anger burned— never a peaceful moment for the heart. Suddenly I decided, as long as we all lived

in one place it would always be thus—until you departed from our native village . . . And so, in the spring of your fifteenth year, I sent you off to distant Edo. (5.74-75)

Issa's first journey into the world was one of exile: sent away by his father for the sake of domestic harmony to seek work in Edo, the Shogun's great city, future Tokyo. According to Issa's recollection, this exile was precipitated by domestic strife between his younger self and his father's second wife, Satsu, whom he depicts as mean and cold-hearted. Although Huey rightly warns that it would be naïve for us to accept at "face value" all that Issa writes about his stepmother and half-brother—after all, he was embroiled in a bitter dispute with them over his inheritance (29)—the theme of abandonment and the image of the orphan crop up so often in his writing throughout his life, he was no doubt deeply scarred by the emotional deprivation, if not outright abuse, of his early years.

In his fifties, he composes this haiku about a motherless sparrow.

我と来てあそぶや親のない雀
ware to kite asobu ya oya no nai suzume
(129.3)

come and play
with me . . .
orphan sparrow

The haiku is one of Issa's most well known. Originally appearing in *Shichiban nikki* ("The Seventh Diary") in First Month, 1814, it is repeated in the 1819 *Oraga haru* with the post-script, "Age six, Yatarō" and a prescript that describes how he was lonely and sad as a child, taunted by village children for being motherless (6.147). He would spend long days by himself, crouched in the shade of the wood pile and reeds behind the garden. His life then, he recalls, was all "grief and sorrow" (6.147). In a different text, he supplies even more details: "A parentless sparrow made himself known by singing pitifully, alone. In a little shack in the back yard, I cared for it all day" (1.129). To call this bird a metaphor seems somehow to dilute the emotional power of the passage. On a deep and real level the sparrow *is* Issa.

The postscript, "Age six, Yatarō," is ambiguous; either this means that the poem is a childhood work, and a remarkably well constructed one at that, or it is a memory-based verse written at age 52. Japanese critics generally assume the latter. Kuriyama explains: "Up to recent years, there was no suspicion [that the haiku was not composed at age six]. However, if one peruses Issa's opus in general, one finds, clearly, this haiku passably fits his mature style. This has been proven by factual inspection" (5). Kobayashi Keiichirō and his fellow editors of *Issa zenshū* agree: "This recollection-of-childhood poem is artificially presented as a childhood work" (6.171).[11]

Issa never forgot the mistreatment and abandonment that propelled him on that first lonely journey in spring of 1777. Stepchildren figure prominently in his work. Sometimes they are birds.

しよんぼりと雀にさへもまま子哉

shonbori to suzume ni sae mo mamako kana
(129.22)

dejected
even among sparrows . . .
a stepchild

又むだに口明く鳥のまま子哉
mata muda ni kuchi aku tori no mamako
kana (126.11)

in vain
the baby bird begs . . .
a stepchild

むだ鳴になくは雀のまま子哉
muda naki ni naku wa suzume no mamako
kana (131.07)

crying its cry
in vain . . .
the stepchild sparrow

夕暮とや雀のまま子松に鳴
yūgure to ya suzume no mamako matsu ni
naku (128.2)

evening falls—
a stepchild sparrow
cries in the pine

Other times, the stepchildren in Issa's poems are human, which makes them even more plainly self-portraits. A recurring theme is the stepchild's shoddy New Year's kite, an emblem of the extent of his new mother's "love."

すすけ紙まま子の凧としられけり
susuke kami mamako no tako to shirare keri
(46.19)

with sooty paper
the stepchild's kite
easy to spot

ままっ子やつぎだらけなる凧
mamakko ya tsugi darake naru ikanobori
(46.24)

the stepchild's
is covered with patches . . .
New Year's kite

まま子凧つぎのいろいろ見へにけり
mamako tako tsugi no iro-iro mie ni keri
(47.1)

the stepchild's kite—
various patches
appear

And when a sold pony glances back at his mother for one last time, anyone familiar with Issa's life story can hardly help but to sense the poet's own childhood sorrow, deeply embedded.

売馬の親かへり見る秋の雨

uri uma no oya kaeri miru aki no ame (465.1)

the sold pony
looks back at his mother . . .
autumn rain

We infer from his poetry that Issa experienced another sort of rejection on his first journey away from home. A farm boy from the provinces, he entered the Shogun's city at a time when governmental authority prefaced its edicts relative to farmers with phrases like, "since peasants are stupid people . . . " and "since peasants are lacking in intelligence and foresight . . . " (Nouet 84). When young Yatarō reached Edo, he encountered the scorn with which the citizens of Edo, the *edokko*, regarded impoverished peasants from the Japanese outback. Though he became a permanent resident, most migrant workers from farm country sought employment in Edo only for the winter months and were called, derisively, *mukudori*, "gray starlings"—perhaps an allusion to the way they swarmed the roads like flocks of migrating birds, as Yuasa suggests (134). Or, as the editors of *Issa zenshū* believe, *mukudori* could be a reference to the plain, shabby clothes worn by the migrants (4.86). Either way, the term is derogatory and cruel, indicating the disdain that the people of Edo harbored for peasants. That such prejudice ran deep is attested in several haiku of Issa's mature years.

椋鳥といふ人さはぐ夜寒哉
mukudori to iu hito sawagu yozamu kana
(436.17)

those who call me "starling"
raise a ruckus . . .
a cold night

椋鳥と我をよぶ也村時雨
mukudori to ware wo yobu nari mura shigure
(628.6)

"A starling from the sticks"
I'm called . . .
winter rain

 椋鳥と人に呼るる寒さ哉
mukudori to hito ni yobaruru samusa kana
(609.5)

"A starling from the sticks!"
he taunts . . .
how cold it is

椋鳥の仲間に入や夕時雨
mukudori no nakama ni iru ya yūshigure
(628.5)

joining the "starlings"
a night of winter
rain

My Japanese advisor Shinji Ōgawa paraphrases
the first haiku, "The people of Edo who call me a

bumpkin are having a good time while I am fighting with the bitter cold of a winter night." The second haiku evokes a similar situation and mood. The third and fourth examples appear back-to-back in an Eleventh Month entry in Issa's journal, 1819, following the prescript, "On the way to Edo" (4.89). Even at age fifty-seven when he was an accomplished poet and haiku teacher, Issa was still viewed as just another peasant cluttering the road in the cold eyes of strangers.

An unwanted stepchild in his native village, a country "starling" in the capital, Issa depicts himself as an aimless, restless wanderer; a bird without a nest . . . homeless. On at least one occasion he was literally so. A fire swept through Edo on New Year's Day, 1809, destroying the house where the poet had been staying (2.559). The following two haiku appear together in *Bunka roku nen ku nikki* ("Bunka Era Sixth Year Haiku Diary," 2.522).

家なしの身に成て見る花[の]春
ie nashi no mi ni natte miru hana [no] haru
(28.11)

homeless now
I view the blossoming
spring

元日や我のみならぬ巣なし鳥
ganjitsu ya waga nominaranu su nashi tori
(23.7)

on New Year's Day
I have company
bird without a nest

Many verses about homeless, abandoned, lost, and traveling animals evoke Issa's own rootless existence. To cite just two more . . .

有明や家なし猫も恋を鳴
ariake ya ie nashi neko mo koi wo naku
(121.4)

at dawn
the homeless cat, too
cries for love

秋の風宿なし鳥吹かれけり
aki no kaze yado nashi karasu fukare keri
(470.17)

in autumn wind
a homeless crow
is blown

Issa is the cat crying for love, the crow drifting through the vast, unfeeling world—a stepchild of a village that rejected him, a country bumpkin in the great capital.

Interestingly, his rootlessness with its origins in the harsh facts of biography becomes something else, something more, in his writing. From the earliest journals Issa self-consciously embraces the persona of a traveling poet-priest, claiming a place in the time-honored tradition of the itinerant Buddhist artist. Specifically, he views himself as a follower of the great haiku poet Bashō, whose literary journeys were legendary. Travel is both a poetic theme and an actual, physically arduous reality for Issa, and on both counts it is properly understood as an expression of Buddhist discipline, as we shall see later in this chapter. Fifteen year-old Kobayashi Yatarō left home in spring 1777. Ten years later, twenty-five year-old Issa surfaced in Edo as a student of Chikua's Nirokuan school of haiku. Three years later, in 1790, when Chikua died, Issa assumed for a brief time the role of master of the school—attesting to his remarkable talent. However, the newly minted haiku poet, who now was signing his work "One Cup-of-Tea" (*Issa:* 一茶), did not settle into a sedentary existence in the Shogun's city. A year later, he took to the open road with travel journal and bamboo brush in hand, setting a pattern for years to come.

He traveled far and wide. Two years after his death, when his students gathered to publish his haiku in an anthology, *Issa hokku shū* ("Issa Haiku Collection"); they singled out in their preface the following verse to epitomize their departed master's life and art.

松蔭に寝てくふ六十よ州かな
matsu kage ni nete kū roku jū yoshū kana
(744.2)

in pine-tree shade
sleeping, eating . . .
sixty provinces!

The students comment: "As for the Old Man, after his 'old pond' there can be no other 'old pond' haiku. And as for Issa, after his 'pine-tree shade,' there can be no other 'pine-tree shade' haiku" (9.215). The "Old Man" is Matsuo Bashō, whose name is forever attached to the words, "old pond/ a frog jumps in/ water sound." Issa's "pine-tree shade" haiku, in similar fashion, makes all other haiku on that subject unnecessary . . . or so his devoted students claim. They admired this haiku so much, they erected a stone monument with an engraving of it in Issa's native village of Kashiwabara on the third-year anniversary of his death (241). Their focus on this particular haiku out of the many thousands that Issa wrote reveals his first audience's first thought about their master. Issa, in the eyes of his disciples, was above all else a traveler—one who slept and dined in the pine-tree shade of "sixty provinces" . . . a euphemism for the entire country of Japan.

He embraced the actual lifestyle as well as the literary persona of the roving poet-priest, preferring the freedom of the mountains to the "cage" of the capital.

鶯は籠で聞かよ閑古鳥
uguisu wa kago de kiku ka yo kankodori
(350.21)

does the caged
nightingale hear?
mountain cuckoo

The free-ranging cuckoo served as Issa's role model for much of his middle years, 1791 to 1813—ages 29 to 51 by traditional Japanese reckoning. Near the end of this far-reaching period of wandering, in 1811, he sums up his first forty-nine years of life in this enigmatic verse.

月花や四十九年のむだ歩き
tsuki hana ya shi jū ku nen no muda aruki
(743.4)

moon! blossoms!
forty-nine years walking
wasted

The poem lacks a clear season word, since it refers both to autumn's harvest moon and the blossoms of spring. The phrase, *tsuki hana ya* ("moon! blossoms!"), suggests the whole cycle of the year—spring to autumn—and, more particularly, the obsessions of the haiku poet, whose life is devoted above all else to the glories of spring blossoms and autumn moon. The opening phrase is exuberant, but then Issa delivers one of his patented haiku surprises: all his years spent wandering under blossoms and moon have been a (wonderful? tragic?) waste: *muda aruki*, a "walk in vain."

His reflections on his own poetic travels are often similarly self-ironic, a precedent that he sets early in his career. In the opening passage of his first travel diary, *Kansei san nen kikō* ("Kansei Era Third Year [1791] Travel Diary"), he caricatures himself as a "mad" drifter: "Rambling to the west, wandering to the east, there is a madman who never stays in one place. In the morning, he eats breakfast in Kazusa; by evening, he finds lodging in Musashi. Helpless as a white wave, apt to vanish like a bubble in froth—he is named Priest Issa" (5.15). His haiku name, "Priest Cup-of-Tea," suggests the constant movement of his lifestyle. Restless Issa has time for just one cup, and then he rushes off. In another early journal, *Chichi no shūen nikki* (1801), he again describes his life using images of restless movement: "Like a floating cloud, thinking to go east then wandering west, with time passing like a wheel rolling down from the top of a hill, twenty five years went by. Until my own head became white as frost, I kept distant from my parent . . . " (75). The "parent" in the passage is Issa's father, who was dying when he wrote this passage. In another entry of this diary, written shortly after his father's death, the bereaved son contemplates his future. He writes that he had promised his father to settle in the family home, but that his stepmother and half brother had raised objections and blocked this from happening. Issa adds, with resignation, that he supposes he will "once again become a Cloud-Water wanderer, hiding in whatever rocky crag or tree-shaded gorge, hating the wind and enduring the rain" (86).

The editors of *Issa zenshū* explain that "Cloud-Water" wanderer (*unsui:* 雲水) refers to an itinerant Buddhist priest, but in this context, it has the particular meaning of a traveling haiku poet (105, note 324). Huey further glosses the term as referring to "wanderers, especially poets, who roamed as freely and easily as clouds (*un*) and water (*sui*)" (54). Issa's adoption of the moniker "priest" and his use of plainly Buddhist terminology to describe his lifestyle of constant motion—west to east, "rocky crag" to "tree-shaded gorge"—suggest that, despite his playfulness and self-irony, he perceived his walk through the world as spiritual discipline, a Buddhist "way." In several self-portraits recorded in his journals, he depicts himself as a walker, a wanderer, a drifting cloud, a stream of water—gliding and unattached. For wandering Cloud-Water priests such as Issa, the refusal to stay in one place made attachment to persons and things difficult; constant movement, as a spiritual exercise, was a means of gaining insight into the transient nature of the universe—our topic for Chapter 4.

Issa did not remain settled in Edo for long after the death of his haiku master Chikua in 1790. In Third Month 1791, at age 29, he left the capital on his first walking tour, meeting with haiku poets in Shimōsa Province, present-day Chiba Prefecture. In *Kansei san nen kikō* he writes, "This third year of Kansei [1791], Third Month, 26th day, leaving Edo behind, I anxiously departed. Frogs in the rice fields were raising a ruckus, the moon over the trees was veiled in mist; right away I set off on my journey" (5.15). This haiku follows.

雉鳴て梅に乞食の世也けり
kiji naite ume ni kojiki no yo nari keri (146.3)

pheasant singing—
it's a plum blossom-filled
beggar's world now!

The phrase, "beggar's world" (*kojiki no yo*), refers to the fact that Issa intended to beg for his meals and lodging along the way. Entering the "beggar's world" of the wandering poet-priest was a happy experience for this caged nightingale finally set free. The Japanese critic, Kaneko Tohta, interprets the mood of this haiku to be one of unbridled joy (26-27). Though a "beggar" now, Issa was rich with plum blossoms and singing pheasants—and ecstatic to be, at long last, following the example of Bashō, whose road journals, particularly his *Oku no hosomichi* ("Narrow Road to the Far Provinces"), provided the model for Issa's own early travel writing.[12]

His 1791 Cloud-Water journey drifted him from Shimōsa to Shinano Province, all the way home to Kashiwabara for the first time in his adult life. The reunion with his father seems to have been a joyful one.

> 門の木も先つつがなし夕涼
> *kado no ki mo mazu tsutsuganashi yūsuzumi*
> (317.27)

> even the tree by the gate
> in good health . . .
> evening cool

As Issa approaches home, the first thing he spots is the old, familiar tree by the gate which, he happily notes, looks healthy. His tone is a hopeful one: Would the father he left behind fourteen years ago be as healthy as the tree? On this first visit, this proved to be the case.

The following year—Third Month, 25th day—Issa headed for the far west and south on a journey to Shikoku and Kyūshū. Leaving Edo, he writes,

> いつ逢ん身はしらぬひの遠がすみ

itsu awan mi wa shiranu hi no tōgasumi
(82.3)

when will we meet again?
I'm off to will-o'-the-wisps
in the far mist.

An excellent illustration of how the spiritual discipline of travel can lead to an appreciation of transience, this haiku has the prescript, "Rain. Before setting off on my journey, saying farewell to the people staying behind" (1.82). This time, Issa was on his way to Shimabara Bay, a place known for *ignis fatuus*: those phosphorescent lights known as "will-o'the-wisps" (Mackenzie 27). The answer to the poem's question ("when will we meet again?") is uncertain in this uncertain world: perhaps one day, perhaps never—one simply doesn't know. Though he feels human attachment to those he leaves behind, his heart lets go . . . and he moves on. In a much later poem (1818) he reflects on the isolation and anonymity of life on the road.

一人と書留らるる夜寒哉
ichi nin to kaki tomeraruru yosamu kana
(437.9)

"A man"
registers at the inn . . .
a cold night

A solitary traveler signs his name, "A man" or "Alone" (*ichi nin* carries both meanings). A stranger without companions, adrift in the universe, he is perfectly poised to realize the fundamental impermanence of that universe, a step toward Buddhist awakening.

By 1793 Issa had reached Shimabara Bay and points beyond, making it all the way to Nagasaki, where, incidentally, he encountered a foreigner.

君が世やから人も来て年ごもり
kimi ga yo ya karabito mo kite toshi-gomori
(684.1)

Great Japan—
a foreigner also attends
the year's end service!

The haiku alludes to the Japanese custom of keeping vigil at a shrine or temple on the year's last day. The opening phrase, *kimi ga yo ya*, literally denotes, "our sovereign's reign" but metaphorically refers to Japan with great patriotic feeling, for it is the opening phrase of the Japanese national anthem: "May our sovereign's reign last for thousands of ages." The scene is quintessentially Japanese, and yet a foreigner (*karabito*) is in attendance as well, most likely a Dutchman (Kuriyama 18). In a "Great Japan" closed off to the outer world, the sight of a European anywhere but in the designated district of Nagasaki, where the Dutch had special permission to trade, was a rarity—so this was probably Issa's first and perhaps only glimpse of a European (Hall 326). Yet instead of difference, he stresses human connection: this foreigner, too, participates in the end-of-year rites.

On that same visit to the south, Issa had another encounter with the foreign.

君が世や茂りの下の那蘇仏
kimi ga yo ya shigeri no shita no yaso-botoke
(420.9)

Great Japan—
overgrown with weeds
Jesus-Buddha

In the previous century, the port of Nagasaki had been the site of a Jesuit mission, until the authorities of "Great Japan" suppressed the foreign cult, crucifying dozens of its followers. Issa contemplates the lone, abandoned "Jesus Buddha." In the first edition of this book, I pictured this to be an old stone cross, but Jean Cholley believes that Issa is actually referring to an image of Jesus disguised as a Buddha, used in an earlier time by clandestine Japanese Christians (234, note 10). With no one clearing away the weeds that have overgrown it, this Jesus-Buddha appears as a forlorn casualty of history and "Great Japan."

In another poignant haiku of 1793, Issa reflects on the isolation of the traveling life.

秋の夜や旅の男の針仕事
aki no yo ya tabi no otoko no harishigoto
(444.19)

autumn evening—
a traveler busy
stitching

He was alone but not a loner. In his years of travel to and fro in the southern islands, he met and hobnobbed with haiku people as often as he could. In Matsuyama City, which to this day remains a center for haiku, he left a lasting impression. In fact, his 1795 visit to a Matsuyama hot spring became the stuff of local legend.

寝ころんで蝶泊らせる外湯哉
ne-koronde chō tomaraseru soto yu kana
(165.9)

lying down
with a visiting butterfly . . .
outer hot spring

This haiku has the prescript, "Close by Dōgo Hot Spring." The hot spring Issa enjoyed that day was an open air pool of overflow water just to the west of Dogo Spa, a place reserved for bathing horses and cattle. This out-of-towner *faux pas* helped to grow his reputation as a good-natured eccentric who cared little about rules of decorum.[13]

Matsuyama's haiku poets embraced their unique visitor, inviting him, in 1796, to participate in a full moon party at the castle on the hill. On the occasion, Issa writes,

人並に畳のうえの月見哉
hito nami ni tatami no ue no tsukimi kana
(454.5)

all in a row
on tatami mats . . .
moon gazing.

Despite such moments of social interaction, life on the road afforded little companionship, unless one counts, as Issa does in 1795, that of the non-human sort.

衣がえ替ても旅のしらみ哉
koromogae kaete mo tabi no shirami kana
(295.2)

summer change of clothes—
but the journey's same
lice

Accompanied only by his lice, Priest Issa drifted through Japan solitary and detached, observing and writing. Even his star, he declares in an 1803 poem, is a traveler.

我星はどこに旅寝や天の川
waga hoshi wa doko ni tabine ya ama no
kawa (448.21)

where will my star
stop for the night?
Heaven's River

According to Japanese folklore, every person, from the moment of birth, is assigned a corresponding star in the heavens. Gazing above at "Heaven' River"—the Milky Way—Issa imagines that his own bright speck amid the celestial glitter must definitely be a wanderer also. He wonders out loud where it might find an inn tonight. In a later, very much related haiku, he asks,

我星は上総の空をうろつくか
waga hoshi wa kazusa no sora wo urotsuku ka (498.5)

sky over Kazusa
is my star up there
prowling?

Through years of practicing the constant movement, isolation, and rootlessness that Buddhist Cloud-Water monks rely on to seek insight into the fleeting nature of things; Issa, not surprisingly, came to understand journeys—important journeys, the journeys that count—as pilgrimages. In one haiku, even a Japanese nightingale (*uguisu*) plays the role of pilgrim.

鶯の毎旦北野参り哉
uguisu no maiasa kitano mairi kana (135.5)

to Kitano
every morning, the nightingale's
pilgrimage

Kitano is a major shrine in Kyoto. The nightingale's daily visit there is described as a religious journey; the bird actively joins the steady stream of human worshippers. In another haiku, a dog tags along with, and becomes one of, the pilgrims on their way to a temple.

法の世は犬さへ十夜参哉
nori no yo wa inu sae jūya mairi kana
(657.24)

world of Buddha's law—
even a dog on winter
pilgrimage

The occasion is the Ten Nights (*jūya*), described by Blyth as a Tenth Month event during which "believers of the Pure Land sect gather at temples and recite the Nembutsu" (*Haiku* 4.1237). As Issa braves the cold weather, trudging through mountains on his way to celebrate Amida Buddha's promise of salvation, he notes, with a warm smile, that the dog, too, is a pilgrim: a manifestation of the universality of "Buddha's law" (*nori*).

To cite just two more examples of this theme, consider these haiku concerning animals and Mount Fuji.

有明や不二へ不二へと蚤のとぶ
ariake ya fuji e fuji e to nomi no tobu (377.9)

dawn—
to Fuji! to Fuji!
fleas jumping off

かたつぶりそろそろ登れ富士の山
katatsuburi soro-soro nobore fuji no yama
(284.13)

little snail
inch by inch, climb
Mount Fuji!

Climbing Mount Fuji in Issa's time was a religious, not recreational, exercise. In Shinto belief, this highest and most sacred of Japan's peaks is the home of great gods. Buddhists of Issa's time believed that it is a mystical gateway between earth and heaven. Perhaps this is why Issa's fleas are impatient to set foot there, hopping—one presumes, off the poet—to begin the sacred climb. The second example refers to an imitation Mount Fuji: a man-made hill in a temple garden. Those who could not climb the real mountain could reap the same karmic benefit by scaling a facsimile, and many of the citizens of Edo did so as part of a Sixth Month observance. In the haiku, a pilgrim snail seems to be earnestly joining in . . . with Issa's encouragement. Miya-mori Asatarō, the first person to critique this haiku in English, writes in 1932, "Needless to say, this is a didactic verse teaching that even a dull-witted man can achieve a great thing with diligence and perseverance. Be slow but sure" (262). While this interpretation acknowledges one level of meaning, it overlooks the spiritual significance of climbing Mount Fuji, real or imitation. Issa's snail, like the nightingale visiting Kitano shrine or the dog at winter prayers, is essentially a pilgrim in this world . . . as is Issa.

Throughout the poet's most rootless years, stepmother Satsu and half brother Senroku continued to oppose his return to Kashiwabara village and the family homestead. The following haiku, composed in 1810, captures the mood of this troubled period.

古郷やよるも障るも茨の花
*furu sato ya yoru mo sawaru mo bara no
hana* (424.16)

the closer I get
to my village, the more pain . . .
wild roses

The people of his native village did not embrace their returning native son, and so he, approaching Kashiwabara, felt pain instead of homecoming joy. In a prescript to this haiku in *Shichiban nikki*, Issa reports that he entered Kashiwabara on the morning of Fifth Month, 19th day, 1810. He paid his respects at his father's gravesite and then met with the village headman. While the content of their meeting is not revealed, it plainly had to do with the matter of Issa's inheritance. He writes, tersely, "After seeing the village elder, entered my house. As I expected they offered me not even a cup of tea so I left there soon" (3.61). In another text dated that same year, he recopies this "wild roses" haiku and signs it, *mamako Issa*: "Issa the Stepchild" (424.16, variant).

The connection between the haiku's middle and last phrases is elusive. Perhaps the roses are simply present in the highland scene, reminding Issa that he is drawing near to the village that does not want to accept him. Or, perhaps, they represent the poet himself, who was always more of an outcast "wild rose" than a cultivated flower. In either case, Stepchild Issa longed to return to Kashiwabara but met fierce opposition.

Fujimoto cites a haiku about wild geese as an example of allegory in Issa's haiku (448). Geese returning from their long migration seem to signify the poet's own homecoming to Kashiwabara.

かしましや江戸見た雁の帰り様
kashimashi ya edo mita kari no kaeri-sama
(152.21)

clamorous—
wild geese who saw Edo
returning home

Like the geese, Issa had seen Edo but now yearned to return to his native place. In Second Month of 1813, at the time of the haiku's composition, he was back in Kashiwabara, living in a rented house, determined to dig in his heels and settle the dispute with Senroku and Satsu once and for all. According to Mackenzie, he threatened to petition the Shogun for a remedy— a risky ploy that led to a swift settlement (37). The family home was divided with a partition wall nailed down the middle, and the stepmother and half brother vacated one side to make room for the returning firstborn. In autumn 1813 he moved in, thus keeping, after twelve years, his promise to his dying father.

Cloud-Water Issa was home, but his Buddhist quest in the world as a man and as an artist was just beginning.

Chapter 2. *NINJŌ:* Human Feeling

According to *Nihon kokugo daijiten* ("The Great Dictionary of the Japanese National Language"), "human feeling" or *ninjō* (人情) is both an essential human trait and an emotion that arises naturally in the hearts and minds of people (15.550). Depending on context, English equivalents of *ninjō* include sympathy, kindness, humanity, and human nature—the latter two translations attributable to the fact that the ability to feel sincerely for others is believed to be an essential ingredient of one's humanity. In Japanese semantics, human beings are feeling beings.

When the Japanese psyche is portrayed in that nation's theater, *ninjō* figures prominently, especially in scenes where it clashes with duty (*giri:* 義理). As Harada notes, *giri* with its sense of chivalry and self-sacrifice normally prevails in such conflicts (693). Human feeling also plays a special role in Buddhist tradition. The historical Buddha's compassion for his fellow beings motivated him in his quest to attain nirvana. In Pure Land mythology, Amida Buddha's infinite compassion prompted him, eons ago, to vow to make a way for sentient beings to be reborn in the Pure Land. Shinran, the founder of the Pure Land sect to which Issa belonged, advocates the bodhisattva ideal: the notion of enlightened saints compassionately returning to the world of suffering to awaken others (*Kyōgyōshinshō* 9). In the Lotus

Sutra, the most popular Buddhist scripture in Japan from medieval times onward, the Universal Buddha is portrayed as a concerned and loving parent determined to save his children from the burning house of worldly attachment (Hurvitz 69-72). In similar fashion, the bodhisattva of mercy, Jizō, is widely venerated in Japan as a saint who works tirelessly to help beings in all Six Realms to achieve rebirth in the Pure Land. As Dykstra observes, this is why statues of him often flank those of Amida Buddha (185).

Issa recognizes the fact that compassion and self-sacrifice for the sake of others are intrinsic to Buddha's mission.

> 人のためしぐれておはす仏哉
> *hito no tame shigurete owasu hotoke kana*
> (624.28, variant)
>
> for our sake enduring
> the winter rain . . .
> Buddha
>
> 誰ためにしぐれておはす仏哉
> *taga tame ni shigurete owasu hotoke kana*
> (624.28)
>
> enduring the winter rain
> for whom?
> stone Buddha

These stone Buddhas endure the cold rain "for the sake of people" (*hito no tame*). In an interesting twist, Issa feels sympathy for the Sympathizer, compassion for the Compassionate One.

The Buddhas appear dejected and forlorn in the icy drizzle, but Issa stops to notice them and, by writing his poems, makes the reader notice too. The feeling is not pity or sappy sentimentality. Issa's heart goes out to the roadside statues in an act of spontaneous, appreciative sympathy that flows from a clear understanding of the Buddha's role, especially in this fallen world and age. The same feeling and understanding pervade this more comic haiku.

野仏の御鼻の先の氷柱哉
no-botoke no o-hana no saki no tsurara kana
(612.20)

from the tip
of the field Buddha's nose . . .
an icicle

The icicle dangling absurdly from the tip of Buddha's nose raises a chuckle, but the compassion of Buddha for the world and Issa for the Buddha should not be missed, or else one misses the poem's deeper resonance. It is out of compassion that the Buddha sits exposed to the elements. Returning that compassion with a reverent bow, Issa utters his poem.

Grateful for their selfless concern for sentient beings, Issa writes often and sympathetically about saints and Buddhas as they are depicted in palpable wood or stone, for example,

びんづるの目ばかり光るけさの雪
binzuru no me bakari hikaru kesa no yuki
(642.22)

like Saint Binzuru's
eyes glittering . . .
this morning's snow.

The bodhisattva Binzuru is one of the Sixteen
Enlightened Ones. According to custom, devotees
who prayerfully rub his image will recover from
illness (Maruyama 223). Yoshida Miwako explains, "In a dark temple, votive lamps darken
Binzuru's image with soot, but his glass eyes still
glitter. It is a pitiful feeling, those glittering eyes
in the gloom" (186). When Issa gazes upon the
morning snow, its twinkle in the gray light
reminds him of Binzuru's eyes in a temple nook.
The resulting haiku is a delicate, nuanced
expression of outer reality (the snow) and inward
feeling (the compassion of, and Issa's compassion
for, the soot-smudged saint).

Issa isn't the only one to feel sympathy for
Buddha in statue form. In New Year's season,
some appreciative soul has spruced up a stone
Buddha with festive decoration.

輪飾や辻の仏の御首へ
wakazari ya tsuji no hotoke no o-kashira e
(38.25)

a New Year's wreath
for the crossroads Buddha's
head

In a summer haiku, another Buddha is similarly
provided for.

石仏誰が持たせし草の花
ishi-botoke tare ga motaseshi kusa no hana
(553.11)

stone Buddha—
who lavished you
with wildflowers?

And in autumn, stone Buddhas are kindly given hats.

御仏も笠きて立や辻踊
mi-botoke mo kasa kite tatsu ya tsuji odori
(496.24)

the Buddha also
with umbrella-hat . . .
crossroads dance

おち栗や仏も笠をめして立
ochi-guri ya hotoke mo kasa wo meshite tatsu
(597.21)

chestnuts dropping—
even the stone Buddha
with umbrella-hat!

The "crossroads dance" (*tsuji odori*) refers to the Bon Festival, at which time people hang lanterns to guide their ancestors' spirits back to the family tombs. The stone Buddha, though his countenance is peaceful and detached, is fully included in the community's celebration, sporting the same umbrella-hat as the dancers. And when chestnuts come pelting down from the trees, some thoughtful passerby provides protective headgear for the Buddha below. In all of these examples, Issa shows not only the Buddha's compassion for sentient beings but human appreciation of, and compassion for, the Buddha.

The compassion of Buddha and saints is not offered only to humans.

雀の子地蔵の袖にかくれけり
suzume no ko jizō no sode ni kakure keri
(128.21)

baby sparrow
safe in Holy Jizō's
sleeve

のら猫が仏のひざを枕哉
nora neko ga hotoke no hiza wo makura kana
(745.17)

the stray cat
makes Buddha's lap
a pillow

大仏の鼻で鳴也雀の子
daibutsu no hana de naku nari suzume no ko
(128.13)

in the great bronze
Buddha's nose chirping . . .
sparrow babies

Jizō provides refuge for a baby sparrow; a stone Buddha in the countryside allows a cat a comfortable lap for deep, protected sleep. In the third example, Issa makes reference to one of two Great Buddha statues of Japan, both cast in bronze: the Kamakura *daibutsu*, an 11.5 meter tall depiction of Amida Buddha, or the even more awesome *daibutsu* that fills the main hall of Todaiji Temple in Nara: a vast Buddha Vairocana topping 16 meters in height (Kobayashi Takeshi 48; Mōri 165). Whichever statue is meant, in the haiku Buddha's dark, cavernous nostril mercifully houses a nest of chirping baby birds. In these poems and countless others, Buddhist *ninjō* is a universal net of compassion that spreads over and embraces all living creatures.

When Issa's nineteenth century commentators, Hyōkai Shisanjin and Seian Saiba, cite *ninjō* as one of his main themes, they allude to the Buddhist connotation of the term: human feeling for the sake of others—spontaneous, natural, selfless. The intensity and pervasiveness of this theme in Issa distinguish him from other masters of haiku tradition; most notably, from his revered predecessor, Bashō. In a revealing passage in one of his travelogues, Bashō describes a scene wherein he happens upon an abandoned three-year-old child crying on the bank of a river. While the great poet feels compassion for the orphan, this emotion is muted by his strict sense of universal order. He uses the occasion to remark sententiously on karma: helping the waif would be out of the question, for who knows what he might have done in an earlier life to deserve his present misery? And so Bashō moves on, leaving the crying child behind (Bashō 52). Issa, one believes, would have behaved differently. Even when a frog is under attack, he gets involved.

痩蛙まけるな一茶是に有り

yasegaeru makeru na issa kore ni ari

(161.11)

scrawny frog, hang tough!
Issa
is here

In more prosaic translation this haiku reads: "Skinny frog, don't be defeated . . . Issa is here." According to prescripts that accompany it in various manuscripts, Issa watched a frog battle on the twentieth day of Fourth Month (1.161). Evidently, a larger, bully frog was getting the better of a scrawnier fellow. Issa refuses to exercise the philosophical restraint of a Master Bashō but instead offers to help his little friend— by shouting his encouragement or else by physically intervening, depending on how one wishes to imagine the scene. Though children delight in the image it paints, the haiku is not *just* a child's poem. The poet's intervention recalls Amida Buddha's concern for sentient beings. Amida relates to his devotees as Issa does to the skinny frog: inspired by *ninjō*, both rescuers fly in from beyond, crashing into the worlds of those being rescued. They do this freely: without coercion and without any reason at all save compassion itself.

In the more secular twentieth century, critics no longer interested in Buddhism began to fixate on Issa's life, convinced that the human feeling in his poetry reflects personal, not cosmic, concerns. Such critics scoured the poet's journals for emotion-packed verses with narrowly biographical connections. Admittedly, Issa to an extent invites this approach by laying bare his heart in many haiku that are as striking for their depth of feeling as they are for their brutal honesty. A famous example is the following.

> 亡母や海見る度に見る度に
> *naki haha ya umi miru tabi ni miru tabi ni*
> (746.24)

> my dead mother—
> every time I see the ocean,
> every time . . .

The rhythmic cadence of the repeated phrase, *miru tabi ni* ("every time I see . . ."), evokes the sad, eternal rush of waves coming in, one after the other. With perfect understatement, the haiku expresses the love and loss felt by a son standing on the shore, alone, remembering his long-dead mother. Biographical critics see this poem in strictly biographical terms. For example, according to Mackenzie, this haiku was inspired by an actual visit to a seashore, where Issa found himself "looking over the changing and changeless pattern of the waves" (11), remembering his mother. Though a Jungian might find a more universal statement in the poem, observing that the mother-ocean connection is a human arche-type, a dim memory, perhaps, of the watery womb; biographical critics of Issa stop at Issa, seeing this haiku and others like it only in terms of his life. This, however, is a mistaken approach, for it leads one to conclude that human feeling in Issa is egocentric and, as such, decidedly un-Buddhist. As mentioned in the introduction, D. T. Suzuki writes off Issa for this very reason, and Suzuki is not alone in his assessment.

A deeper study of Issa's "mother/ocean" haiku suggests that its content and feeling, though grounded in biography and self-interest, tran-scend them both. In *Shichiban nikki*, it is followed immediately by another ocean piece that provides a vital clue as to *which* ocean Issa is contem-plating.

紫の雲にいつ乗るにしの海
murasaki no kumo ni itsu noru nishi no umi
(743.10)

on purple clouds
when will I set sail?
western sea

At the time of composition, Third Month 1812, Issa was staying in the vicinity of the capital, far from the physical western sea that separates Japan from China. In any case, he is not referring in this poem or in the preceding one to a physical ocean but rather to the mythic "western sea" that separates this world from Amida's Pure Land. The haiku might be paraphrased: "When will purple clouds of glory carry me off to the Western Paradise?" Viewing Issa's "dead mother" haiku in the context of this next one in his journal, one might reasonably conclude that the ocean in question is, at least on one level, the gulf between this world and the next, the barrier that divides the living from those who have passed on.[14]

Issa is a Buddhist artist with an expansive, generous, all-embracing, and compassionate worldview—not the whining egotist that some have made him out to be. Though scores of his haiku visions grow from deeply personal, real-life situations, they just as plainly evoke universal significance. Like the Romantic poets of England who were his contemporaries, Issa's self comes to serve as a central metaphor in his writing: the abandoned stepchild, the "chief beggar of Shinano Province," the indolent napper while others labor in the fields, the Cloud-Water drifter, the quirky iconoclast unconcerned with secular power and feudal hierarchy . . . such carefully crafted self-portraits reveal an Everyman whose private joys and sorrows broaden in relevance as they are artistically transformed on the page. Even the most overtly biographical of his poems resonate with universal significance. A prime example is a strange haiku about a house divided.

春立や二軒つなぎの片住居
haru tatsu ya ni ken tsunagi no kata sumai
(31.12)

spring begins—
two houses adjoined
one home

Without knowledge of certain facts of Issa's biography, the poignancy of this verse is lost on the reader. The house in question is the family home in Kashiwabara village, the home over which Issa struggled bitterly with his stepmother and half brother. As we noted earlier, the village headman finally ended the dispute by ordering that a wall be constructed, dividing one home into two. Once the reader understands its context, the haiku's emotional power is revealed. Two families living under the same roof, separated by a thin wall, greet the new year, new spring, separately.[15] However, they might as well be thousands of miles apart, such is the gulf represented by that wall. The haiku, then, makes a broad statement about *ninjō*'s defeat: the willful separation of people who have broken the connection that should bind them. Issa's intimately personal experience becomes a window into a tragically recurring human theme.

Since biography colors so many of Issa's haiku, it is tempting to declare biographical connections throughout his writing, even where textual support for such attribution is lacking. Two of the early English translator/critics of Japanese haiku, Harold Henderson and R. H. Blyth, fall into this trap more than once. For example, Henderson claims that this next haiku alludes to Issa's dying wife.

鳴な虫別るる恋はほしにさへ

naku na mushi wakaruru koi wa hoshi ni sae
(501.12)

> don't cry, insects—
> lovers part
> even among the stars

The seasonal setting is the Festival of Tanabata, the seventh night of Seventh Month. According to Japanese legend, it is the one night of the year during which two starry lovers parted by Heaven's River (the Milky Way) can cross the bridge and be reunited. Henderson comments: "It has an effect of lightness, perhaps even of over-sentimentality toward the insects. But from Issa's diary one learns that when it was written Issa's dearly loved wife, Kiku, was lying in her last illness, and once again Issa is tearing his heart out before us" (133). This haiku appears in the diary *Bunsei kuchō* ("Bunsei Era Haiku Notebook")—a Seventh Month entry for the year 1822. Despite Henderson's claim, Kiku did not fall into her "last illness" until the following year, on the 19th day of Second Month, 1823. She passed away three months thereafter (Kobayashi Keiichirō 263). Issa's haiku about insects crying for mates could not possibly refer to the loss of his wife. In fact, it seems to have no personal or biographical connection whatsoever.[16]

Blyth makes a similar error when he speculates that the following haiku has a special, personal meaning to Issa.

> 生残り生残りたる寒[さ]哉
> *ikinokori ikinokoritaru samu[sa] kana*
> (607.22)

surviving
and surviving . . .
how cold it is!

Blyth translates the second phrase, *ikinokitaru*, as: "Outliving them all," and goes on to explain, "This was written when Issa's wife died, he being 61. His fourth child had died just before, and he himself was stricken with the palsy" (*Haiku* 1.366). The year that Blyth is describing is 1823, but the haiku in question was actually written twelve years earlier, in 1811, long before the deaths of Issa's children and wife, back when he was still a bachelor.

In Blyth's defense, he did not have access, in the late 1950s and early 1960s, to the authoritative complete works of Issa, the first volume of which came out in 1979. Perhaps, then, he was swayed in his interpretation of this "surviving" haiku by an earlier one that is unequivocally biographical. In *Chichi no shūen nikki*, the following verse marks the day that Issa ritually gathered up his father's ashes.

生残る我にかかるや草の露
ikinokoru ware ni kakaru ya kusa no tsuyu
(474.4)

I, who outlived him
in the dewy
field

Dewdrops, a conventional symbol of impermanence, remind the mourning poet of the dear life that has passed away. While this 1801 haiku clearly refers to the human feeling stirred by the loss of a loved one, this cannot be said about the 1811 poem.

Though readers are eternally in their debt for their efforts to introduce Japanese haiku to the West, Henderson and Blyth made errors in their haste to match particular poems to particular circumstances of Issa's life. Sadly, the biographical approach can mislead even when critics have their facts straight. There is no doubt that Issa poetically associates his own childhood abandonment with orphan sparrows. Nevertheless, to read such poems as *merely* about his life limits their meaning and ignores their more universal connotations.

夕暮や親なし雀何と鳴
yūgure ya oya nashi suzume nanto naku
(127.24)

evening—
how the orphan sparrow
cries!

鳴よ鳴よ親[な]し雀おとなしき
nake yo nake yo oya [na]shi suzume
otonashiki (127.20a)

sing, sing!
orphan sparrow . . .
so quiet

If we regard such sparrows as merely masks for

Issa, the content of these haiku appears self-absorbed; the tone, self-pitying. However, beyond their biographical connection to the poet, the sparrows in such haiku are actual birds for whom Issa feels tenderly, inviting the reader to do the same. Imbued with generous compassion—selfless *ninjō*, not selfish sorrow—such "motherless sparrow" poems reveal something bigger than biography, something about the human condition: all of us, at one time or another, have found or will find ourselves alone and abandoned in the vast world.

If orphan sparrows represent the poet in his haiku, what are we to make of sparrows that appear with intact families?

むつまじき二親もちし雀哉
mutsumajiki futaoya mochishi suzume kana
(127.23)

sweet harmony—
the sparrow has
both parents!

親雀子雀山もいさむぞよ
oya suzume ko suzume yama mo isamu zoyo
(128.03)

parent sparrows
baby sparrows . . .
a happy mountain

雀子や親のけん［嘩］をしらぬ顔
suzume-go ya oya no ken[ka] wo shiranu kao
(128.05)

baby sparrow—
his face unaware
of his parents' fights

If such poems are read with one's mind fixed on
Issa's unpleasant childhood, their playfulness
and joy are lost, much like the scene of a happy
Christmas feast saddens the homeless person
outside the window, looking in. It is myopic and
not in keeping with Issa's generous character to
see his sparrows in this way. In his haiku, his
sparrows are first and foremost—concretely,
palpably—sparrows. The human feeling that he
extends to them, whether they have happy parents, bickering parents, or no parents at all; is
best expressed with the Japanese term, *ninjō*.

Before we leave the topic of baby sparrows and
human feeling, this haiku deserves mention.

牢屋から出たり入ったり雀の子
rōya kara detari ittari suzume no ko (130.20)

flying in and out
of the prison . . .
baby sparrows

The prisoners are unseen, but we feel their
presence—and feel *for* them. Issa brilliantly juxta-

poses bondage and freedom, guilt and innocence, stasis and movement, sorrow and joy, society and Nature. The baby sparrows flit easily over walls and through barred windows, but the human beings inside know no such freedom. With deft understatement Issa intimates pathos in the scene. He says nothing overt about emotion yet gently tugs at the reader's heartstrings.

Though Higginson claims that Issa "had a rather pessimistic view of human nature" (16), he wrote many haiku in which human beings freely exhibit the *ninjō* that confirms their humanity. A quintessential example is the following.

旅人や野にさして行流れ苗
tabi-bito ya no ni sashite yuku nagare nae
(405.18)

the traveler fixes
the farmer's floating
rice stalks

In summer rice is transplanted, stalk by stalk, from the seedling beds to flooded paddies. A traveler, walking along, notices some stalks floating loose and, in an act of spontaneous kindness, stops to stick them back into the mud so that they can grow.[17] He receives no extrinsic reward for his impromptu field work: he will not be around when the rice is harvested, nor will the farmer even stroke his ego with a thank-you. The human feeling embodied in his simple action is utterly selfless: he replants the rice for the sake of a stranger and, just as importantly, for the sake of the rice plants themselves—a life-loving gesture that recalls the Buddhist ideal of compassion for sentient beings and, more anciently, the Taoist concept of "superior virtue." As Lao Tzu observes in Chapter 38 of *Tao Te Ching*, "Superior humanism acts but has no private ends to serve" (Cheng 130).[18]

Issa's poetry is replete with scenes that reveal *ninjō* in its selfless, spiritual aspect. Small acts of generosity and concern abound in his haiku, casting doubt on the thesis that he was embittered or pessimistic about humankind.

> 大根引大根で道を教へけり
> *daikon hiki daikon de michi wo oshie keri*
> (726.1)

> with a just-yanked
> radish
> pointing the way

> 菜畠を通してくれる十夜哉
> *na-batake wo tōshite kureru jūya kana*
> (657.11)

> he lets me cross
> his field . . .
> night of winter prayers

The first haiku is one of Issa's most widely translated and admired poems. In it, the farmer has just pulled a *daikon,* a large radish, which he uses as a prop while giving directions. This simple gesture for the sake of a stranger resonates with *ninjō.* The same can be said of the farmer's action in the second haiku. During the winter Festival of Ten Nights, the faithful make pilgrimages to temples, where they chant the *nembutsu,* a prayer of gratitude for Amida Buddha's saving grace. This grace, the pilgrims believe, will enable their rebirth in the harmonious Pure Land where each of them will attain enlightenment. In Issa's poem the farmer's compassion momentarily remedies the world's depravity. When he allows a pilgrim to cut through his precious field, ego is laid aside and some piece of the Pure Land is glimpsed, in the haiku, here and now.

A discussion of human feeling in Issa would not be complete without mentioning his sympathetic and heartfelt depictions of the dregs of society: outcasts, beggars, and prostitutes.

> えた村や山時鳥ほととぎす
> *eta mura ya yama hototogisu hototogisu*
> (338.22)

> an outcast village
> in the mountains . . .
> "cuckoo! cuckoo!"

> 時鳥橋の乞食も聞れけり
> *hototogisu hashi no kojiki mo kikare keri*
> (339.5)

a cuckoo—
the bridge beggar
listens too

木がらしや二十四文の遊女小家
kogarashi ya ni jū shi mon no yūjo koya
(632.22)

cold wind—
a twenty four cent
prostitute shack

The outcasts in the first poem are the *eta*, today called the *burakumin*. In feudal times the members of this lowest of social classes performed "unclean" tasks such as disposing of dead livestock, crafting leather, and executing criminals. They were subjected to harsh racial apartheid, scorned by "pure" Japanese. Nevertheless, in the haiku the citizens of the outcasts' village, like the bridge beggar in the second example, are just as blessed as an emperor when it comes to Nature's gifts—in this case, the mellifluous warbling of a Japanese cuckoo (*hototogisu*) in summer. The women in the third poem, however, enjoy no such natural succor. The bitter-cold wind blasts their little house, and readers must imagine for themselves what life is like for those who live, and sell their bodies, inside. The editors of *Issa zenshū* describe them as "the lowest grade of prostitute" in the Edo period's hierarchy of this trade (6.174). Because they are unseen, we feel their humanity, destitution, and isolation all the more—and we sense Issa's compassion as well.

From its inception Pure Land Buddhism attracted social outcasts—ordinary sinners who, despite or because of their sins, turned to the *nembutsu* prayer in hope of attaining rebirth in the Western Paradise. The patriarch Hōnen, Shinran's teacher, welcomed fishermen, samurai, thieves, and prostitutes to the faith (Bloom, *Life of Shinran* 9). Issa's sympathetic treatment of social and religious outcasts accords perfectly with Pure Land tradition. He sketches a thief with non-judgmental warmth.

梁上の君子も見やれ草の露
ryōjō no kunshi mo mi yare kusa no tsuyu
(483.4)

a robber looks too—
ah! dewdrops
in the grass

And *ninjō* permeates his portrait of rain pouring into a beggar's box.

重箱の銭四五文や夕時雨
jūbako no zeni shi go mon ya yū shigure
(628.3)

in the box
four or five pennies . . .
night of winter rain

This poem appears in *Hachiban nikki* with the prescript, "Temple courtyard beggar" (4.85). When Issa recopied it in *Oraga haru*, he lengthened the prescript: "Taking pity on a beggar at Zenkōji's gate" (6.155). These prose introductions clarify whose box of coins is at issue on this night of winter rain. In the haiku, Issa allows the reader an intimate glimpse into the naked core of the beggar's world: a box with its pittance of coins. Without saying anything directly about his own feelings, Issa's compassion, his *ninjō*, is palpable.

In another haiku, a mother wraps herself protectively around her child.

母親を霜よけにして寝た子哉
haha oya wo shimoyoke ni shite neta ko kana (697.14)

Mother
is the frost-guard . . .
sleeping child

In *Hachiban nikki*, Issa prefaces this verse with a prescript: "Beggar on a bridge" (4.152). The beggar mother is a good mother, sacrificing her own comfort so that her child may sleep. In a similar portrayal of maternal love, a mother eats the astringent parts of a persimmon.

渋[い]所母が喰けり山の柿
shibu[i] toko haha ga kui keri yama no kaki (590.2)

Mother eats
the astringent part . . .
mountain persimmon

Blyth cites this haiku as an example of a Zen Buddhist love of the universe, "the end and aim and consummation of our pilgrimage here" (*Haiku* 1.231). However, since Issa did not follow the Zen sect, the poem might more aptly be understood in the context of Jōdoshinshū, Shinran's True Teaching Pure Land faith. The mother's selfless love for her child reflects Amida Buddha's selfless compassion.

Though Ōshiki Zuike titled his 1984 book about Issa, "The Sorrow of Life" (*Jinsei no hiai*: 人生の悲哀), it is a mistake to typecast the poet as a sufferer obsessed with abandonment and personal grief. On the whole, the human feeling that saturates his haiku is of the non-clinging, selfless, resigned, generous, and spontaneous sort. Like the traveler who replants the farmer's floating rice stalks, Issa expresses unsolicited sympathy for his fellow creatures, human and non-human, without ego gratification or the expectation of personal reward. Even when his attention turns to his own life's tragedies—the loss of a father, a mother, and, as we will see later, children—the feeling in such poems is always universal, always more than one man's personal grumbling. He transforms his private experience into public art that he graciously shares with the world, for which reason his writing itself can be viewed as an act of loving generosity or, as his countrymen would call it, *ninjō*. Such compassionate feeling for others comprises an essential value of Pure Land Buddhism: the heart of the historical Buddha's teaching, Amida Buddha's grace, and all the selfless ministrations of Jizō and the millions of other bodhisattvas—and bodhisattva poets—at work in this world.

Chapter 3. *SETAI:* The State of the World

In Pure Land Buddhist belief, the present age of *mappō* (末法) is the third and worst of three ages that followed the historical Buddha's entrance into nirvana. First came the age of Right Dharma (*shōbō:* 正法) during which Buddhist teaching, practice, and enlightenment all existed. According to Shinran, this golden age lasted five hundred years. Next came a millennium of Imitative Dharma (*zōbō:* 象法), when only teaching and practice were possible, not enlightenment. The present, third age of *mappō*, the "Latter Days of Dharma," comprises a ten thousand year period of corruption in which only Buddhist teaching survives; practice and enlightenment are unattainable through ego-corrupted self-power (*jiriki:* 自力). In this depraved time, clerics who faithfully follow Buddha's precepts are, as one commentator puts it, "rare as a tiger in the marketplace" (Jaffe 129). Shinran regards self-powered faith as an oxymoron. In the Latter Days of Dharma, he insists, only the "Other Power" (*tariki:* 他力) of Amida Buddha can bring about rebirth in the Pure Land, where enlightenment is possible.

Worldly corruption is a favorite theme for Issa from his earliest period on. In his travel journal of 1791, *Kansei san nen kikō*, he laments, "In this corrupt world of today . . . those who are rich have no heirs; those who have children are poor with nothing to leave them; if there's a mountain, it lacks water; if there's a village, it lacks trees; to have both a mountain and fresh water is rare, indeed" (5.16). This world, in Issa's poetic imagination, is a tainted and tainting place. Perfection is impossible, as shown in a haiku about Waka-no-Ura, a seacoast of legendary beauty.

掃溜に鶴の下りけり和歌の浦
hakidame ni tsuru no ori keri waka no ura
(744.21)

a crane lands
on the rubbish heap . . .
Waka-no-Ura

This harshly ironic haiku appears in Issa's journal in a Ninth Month, 1820 entry. The crane, a noble bird and emblem of long life, perfectly accords with the postcard image of this most poetic of seaside locales. However, the fetid rubbish heap that it lands upon pops the romantic bubble. A month later, in the same journal, the poet revises to capture an even more jarring juxtaposition.

掃溜も鶴だらけ也和歌の浦
hakidame mo tsuru darake nari waka no ura
(744.22)

the cranes swarm
the rubbish heap . . .
Waka-no-Ura

This rewrite presents the Old Japanese equivalent of seagulls at a landfill, flapping and squawking and fighting for morsels. Waka-no-Ura may be the loveliest of earthly places, but today its "noble" cranes greedily swarm its garbage.

These Waka-no-Ura haiku are typical examples of Issa's poetic joke telling, showing his delight in irony and incongruity: the clash of romantic ideal and gritty real. But viewed in light of the Pure Land Buddhist understanding of *mappō*, these poems make a serious point. In another comic haiku, this one about air pollution, Issa again creates humor with grave implications.

はつ蛍都の空はきたないぞ
hatsu hotaru miyako no sora wa kitanai zo
(359.8)

first firefly—
the sky over the capital
is smoggy!

The sky over the capital is *kitanai*, "unclean"; the poor firefly must endure the smog that humans have spewed. The second half of the haiku, "the sky over the capital/ is smoggy!" can be read as Issa's warning to the firefly or the firefly's complaint to Issa. Either way, natural beauty has once again been defiled by human activity, and this defilement, again, can be understood in Buddhist terms. The rubbish at Waka-no-Ura and the dirty air over imperial Kyoto are merely outward signs of an invisible, deadlier, and more insidious phenomenon: the human ego's drive to control that which cannot be controlled, to grasp that which should be let go. People spoil things: seacoasts, skies, and, above all, their own efforts to attain enlightenment. Selfish striving produces garbage, stench, and an inability of detaching one's self, by one's own efforts, from earthly addictions.

In these next two haiku, worldly corruption affects even the gods.

苦のさばや神の御立も雨嵐
ku no saba ya kami no o-tatsu mo ame arashi
(656.17)

world of suffering—
when the gods travel, too
a storm

人の世は月もなやませたまいけり
hito no yo wa tsuki mo nayamase tamai keri
(462.12)

world of man—
even the moon
suffers!

In Shinto belief, on the first day of Tenth Month the local gods of Japan leave their shrines to gather at the Great Shrine of Izumo-Taisha. In this "world of suffering," Issa imagines, the pilgrim gods must plod miserably to their great convocation through a winter storm. The second example refers to the harvest moon eclipse of 1819. Alluding to a popular belief that lunar eclipses indicate that the moon is sick, Issa suggests that the cause of its malady is this "world of man" (*hito no yo*), a phrase that suggests the fallen age of *mappō* and its human origin. In Issa's Jōdoshinshū vision, even the divine moon

on this most auspicious night suffers from con-
tamination by the human world. The eclipse in
question took place on Eighth Month, 15th Day—
October 3, 1819 on the Western calendar. In
Hachiban nikki, Issa describes the event with
astronomical precision: "Clear skies. At Inachō's
house. A lunar eclipse, around the time of Hog [9-
11 p.m.], began on the left side. In the 6th period
of Rat [12:30-12:45 a.m.], total eclipse. In the 5th
period of Ox [2:15-2:30 a.m.], all done; the
darkness moved off to the right" (4.67).

This 1819 dimming of the harvest moon inspired several other haiku that allude to worldly
corruption, including these.

> 人の世へ月[も]出直し給ひけり
> *hito no yo e tsuki [mo] denaoshi tamai keri*
> (462.11)

> to the world of man
> the moon deigns
> to return

> 名月も出直し給ふ浮世哉
> *meigetsu mo denaoshi tamau ukiyo kana*
> (462.14)

> the harvest moon
> deigns to return . . .
> floating world!

> 人顔は月より先へ欠にけり
> *hito kao wa tsuki yori saki e kake ni keri*
> (462.9)

people's faces vanish
before
the moon does[19]

The first two poems have similar structure and convey roughly the same idea. The moon deigns to return to the "world of man" (*hito no yo*) in the first, while in the second it returns to the "floating world" (*ukiyo*). The latter expression should not be confused with the colorful and urbane *ukiyo-e* style of Edo period painting. Issa uses "floating world" in its older Buddhist sense, denoting the world's impermanence and imperfection. In this light, the moon's return is an act of supreme generosity, reminiscent of the bodhisattva ideal. Just as awakened saints compassionately return to the suffering world to lead others to enlightenment, the moon returns and *literally* enlightens, sending down divine beams to bathe all below who have had the patience—and faith—to wait and watch. The third haiku indicates that some of the moon-gazers have lacked such patience. They have not kept vigil for the duration of the eclipse, missing the moon's complete darkening and its grand return in the early morning hours. People's faces vanish before the moon's face does: a comic statement that brings focus to the imperfection of the sublunary "world of man."

Just as it can make the moon lose its light, the world in the age of *mappō* distorts the splendors of Nature, bending lotuses and warping dewdrops.

咲花も此世の蓮はまがりけり

saku hana mo kono yo no hasu wa magari keri (399.12)

this world's
blooming lotuses
are bent

蓮の葉に此世の露はいびつ也
hasu no ha ni kono yo no tsuyu wa ibitsu nari (480.27)

on lotus leaves
this world's dewdrops
are warped

The phrase "this world" (*kono yo*), like "world of man" (*hito no yo*) and "floating world" (*ukiyo*), conjures for Pure Land Buddhists the idea of *mappō*. In Japanese Buddhist semantics, a diametrical opposition exists between the soiled world of the present era and Amida Buddha's dazzlingly ideal Western Paradise. In the Pure Land, according to the tenth-century patriarch Genshin, "Palaces, halls, forests, and ponds shine and glitter everywhere"; all who are fortunate enough to cross the "sea of suffering" and be reborn there find themselves bedecked with dazzling jewels, sitting upon lotus-seats (Tsunoda 197). Shinran, in the thirteenth century, also imagines Paradise as a place of shining, perfect, "Boundless Light." Yet in "this world," Issa notes, lotuses are bent and their leaves warp the dew. Such laments about the corrupt, suffering world suggest an unspoken, poignant longing for its faraway opposite, Amida's Pure Land. Perhaps this is why, in another dewdrop poem, the dew-drops themselves seem eager for extinction.

露ちるやむさい此世に用なしと
tsuyu chiru ya musai kono yo ni yō nashi to
(477.21)

dewdrops scatter—
"Goodbye, cruel
world!"

In more literal translation, the scattering dew-drops declare themselves done with "this foul world" (*musai kono yo*). In Buddha's Paradise, the pearl-like drops would be, literally, pearls, having transcended the world of impermanence. Here, however, their existence is short and their beauty distorted. When they talk, for Issa allows them to do so, they register a last, dying, cosmic com-plaint.

Issa is not as pessimistic as the dewdrops he gives voice to; his comic tone suggests that he is smiling, not frowning, at their predicament, which is the same for all beings, including human ones. In another haiku even the blooming cherry trees find themselves sucked into the vortex of worldly depravity, yet, once again, the tone is humorous.

苦の娑婆や桜が咲ば咲いたとて
ku no shaba ya sakura ga sakeba saita tote
(232.13)

world of pain—
and the cherry blossoms
add to it![20]

We are not told *how* the blossoms are adding to the pain of existence; perhaps Issa is annoyed by the hordes of flower-viewers invading the cherry grove—a theme of other haiku.[21] Or, his focus might be on the blossoms' transience: how they fade and scatter so quickly, representing yet another painful loss in a world in which everything good and beautiful (and bad and ugly, for that matter) dies. Whatever particular idea lurks in this mysterious haiku, two things seem certain: (1) it is predicated on the Buddhist concept of worldly depravity in the Latter Days of Dharma, and (2) its odd claim that cherry blossoms cause pain makes for comedy, not tragedy. This doesn't mean that Issa lacks sincerity in his appreciation of Pure Land eschatology. What he finds funny and worthy of a chuckle is the conscious effort to struggle against the universe or complain about it, even when the complainer is himself.

In Issa's poetic vision worldly corruption is nowhere more evident than in the human heart. When lightning flashes, he catches sight of it in people's faces.

稲妻や狗ばかり無欲顔

inazuma ya enokoro bakari muyoku kao

(485.16)

lightning flash—
only the puppy's face
is innocent

Covetousness (*yoku*) pervades the world; Issa perceives this in the faces of the men or women illumined by the sudden flash. The puppy's face, however, appears *muyoku*, "without covetousness." Human beings fail the lightning test. In a thematically related haiku, Issa observes, laconically,

人はいさ直な案山子もなかりけり

hito wa isa suguna kagashi mo nakari keri
(512.8)

like people
an upright scarecrow
can't be found.

The pun works in English as well as in Japanese. Scarecrows are not "upright" in that they do not stand straight; people are not "upright" morally.

As we have noted, Issa shows people spoiling seacoasts with their rubbish and skies with their smog. They even, at times, spoil flowers—or at least attempt to—once again proving to be active agents in the degeneracy of the age.

人間がなくば曲らじ菊の花

ningen ga nakuba magaraji kiku no hana
(558.15)

> if it weren't for people
> they'd not grow crooked . . .
> mums

This haiku might be paraphrased, "If there were no people, there would be no bending of the chrysanthemum flowers."[22] Issa alludes here to the practice of tying and contorting chrysanthemums so that they grow in all sorts of wildly crooked ways, sacrificing their natural form to the gardener's whimsy. If people and scarecrows do not stand "upright" in this world, neither do mums, thanks to human meddling.

Despite his Pure Land Buddhist appreciation of humanity's essential, ego-driven corruption in the age of *mappō*, Issa was no misanthrope. Throughout his poetry and journals he adopts the rhetorical stance of an outsider, creating for himself the comic persona of "Shinano Province's Chief Beggar," then using this distancing of himself from his more worldly comrades to poke gentle fun at them, not to condemn.

> おらが世やそこらの草も餅になる
> *oraga yo ya sokora no kusa mo mochi ni naru*
> (109.20)

> my world—
> those herbs over yonder
> become my cake

In two texts, this haiku has the prescript, "Noblemen delight in the moon and grieve for the [fallen] blossoms" (1.109). Issa, with a wink, delights in the fact that he is no nobleman: humble weeds are plenty good enough to become his "rice cake" (*mochi*). This proletarian outlook has endeared Issa to readers who embrace him as a champion of the working man and woman. When a bill collector enters a farmer's house, it is easy to tell where Issa's sympathies lie.

掛取が土足ふみ込むいろり哉
kaketori ga dosoku fumi-komu irori kana
(666.11)

the bill collector
with shoes on steps inside . . .
to the hearth

Ignoring the Japanese custom of removing his footwear, the agent of class oppression stomps rudely into the house to warm himself at its hearth. The winter cold outside is not nearly as cold as the heart of this invader. The image is stark, and yet it emerges, oddly, from *ninjō:* "Beggar Issa" feels warm solidarity with the poor, oppressed farmer and from this human feeling writes his poem.

His belief in the fundamental corruption of the "world of man" explains why Issa always seems so utterly unimpressed by the men who run that world.

鶯や御前へ出ても同じ声
uguisu ya gozen e dete mo onaji koe (138.11)

nightingale
for the emperor too . . .
the same song

Spring's nightingale warbles the same for rich and poor, oppressor and oppressed. Its song cannot be bought, commanded, meddled with, or taxed. It is one of Nature's gifts to the beauty-loving human spirit, and, as such, suggests a realm of being beyond feudal hierarchy and class warfare. Into this age of unbridled covetousness and state-enforced inequality the nightingale injects something so pure (as in "Pure Land") that its attentive listeners temporarily escape the strictures of society and the roles they play in it. The nightingale sings with the "same voice" (*onaji koe*) for the emperor and for everyone else. In similar fashion, Issa, the "beggar" poet from the mountains, does not change his tune to suit different audiences. His poetic art and the messages woven therein are the same for all readers, regardless of social standing.

Nature's gifts make a poor man equal to a feudal lord.

反古凧や隣は前田加賀守
hogo-dako ya tonari wa maeda kaga no kami
(46.10)

a wastepaper kite
next to that of Maeda
Lord of Kaga!

The Lord of Kaga ruled Issa's home province of Shinano, where farmers loathed his rice tax as much as they feared his armed force that ensured their payment of it. The kite that bears the great daimyo's crest flies no higher than the waste-paper one flown by some commoner—perhaps by Issa. Nature not only ignores class distinctions, it renders them meaningless. Similar poems about kites and the juxtaposition of rich and poor appear in the journals, including these.

今様の凧上りけり乞食小屋

ima yō no tako nobori keri kojiki goya (45.10)

a trendy kite soars
a beggar's shack
below

乞食子や歩ながらの凧

kojiki ko ya aruki nagara no ikanobori (46.17)

a beggar child
walking and flying
a kite

Though they have little, beggars at least have the wind to lift their New Year's kites into the sky. Nature blesses all.

乞食小屋富のおちけり春の雨

kojiki goya tomi no ochi keri haru no ame (74.2)

on a beggar's shack
riches fall . . .
spring rain

貧乏人花見ぬ春はなかりけり
bimbōnin hana minu haru wa nakari keri
(210.1)

for the poor
there's not a spring
without blossoms!

薮超の乞食笛よ鶯夜よ
yabu goshi no kojjiki fue yo uguisu yo (136.3)

wafting through trees
a beggar's flute
a nightingale

If each drop of spring rain is a precious gift, the beggar in his broken-down shack is a millionaire. Trees and flowers bloom every year for people of all classes, including the lowest, as we are reminded in the second haiku. In the third, feudal hierarchy has nothing to do with one's ability to harmonize with Nature. Sweet music is sweet music. The beggar and the nightingale combine forces in a spontaneous duet. In similar fashion, a beggar and a courtier can unite in their music.

玉琴も乞食の笛もかすみけり
tamagoto mo kojiki no fue mo kasumi keri
(83.24)

a precious harp
a beggar's flute
deep in mist

Returning to the topic of feudal lords, we see in this well-known verse that Nature literally knocks one off his high horse.

大名を馬からおろす桜哉
daimyō wo uma kara orosu sakura kana
(234.9)

a lord
forced off his horse . . .
cherry blossoms

Though it has the prescript, "Ueno"—referring to the prime blossom-viewing district of Edo—this haiku was composed in Shinano Province during a snowy Second Month in 1810 (4.470). The scene, then, is imagined or remembered. Either way, it has historical resonance. The first Tokugawa Shogun, Tokugawa Ieyasu, was enshrined at Ueno (in addition to his more grandiose shrine at Nikko). At the foot of Ueno hill, a "Dismount Your Horse" placard was posted (Maruyama 344, note 1860); the daimyo's dismounting in Issa's haiku thus accords with local law. However, it also operates as a richly symbolic image: the "worthless" beauty of Ueno's cherry blossoms humbling the great feudal lord. As Henderson explains, this ironic haiku describes a startling role reversal: normally, common folk are the ones who are "forced" off of their horses to grovel at the roadside when a daimyo passes (128). Today, however, the daimyo plays the peasant's role, suggesting that Nature's power trumps the human kind. The cherry blossoms command no armies of samurai, yet their fragile beauty teaches the daimyo, the observing poet, and the reader an unforgettable lesson in true power, the kind of power that really, ultimately, counts.

More oblique and subtle critiques of worldly status in a worldly age can be found in Issa's poetry. The following haiku might not seem satirical at first glance.

大名と肩並べけりきくの花
daimyō to kata narabe keri kiku no hana
(563.4)

neck and neck
with the mighty lord . . .
chrysanthemum

The flower and the daimyo have equal stature: a statement of fact from which, if the reader chooses, more can be inferred. The feudal lord doesn't lord over the mum. The reader must work even harder to get the political gist of this next example.

鶯や泥足ぬぐふ梅の花
uguisu ya doro ashi nuguu ume no hana
(134.14)

nightingale wipes
his muddy feet . . .
plum blossoms

Anita Virgil notes that the plum blossom is the emblem of the Maeda family, and so this poem can be viewed as a "veiled jab" at the Lord of Kaga (139). The nightingale ignores tokens of human status, wiping his muddy feet wherever he likes, even on the Maeda family symbol. Though some readers may find Virgil's plum blossoms/Lord of Kaga association a bit of a stretch, Issa was certainly aware of the daimyo's connection to plum blossoms, as evidenced in the following haiku that appears in one of his diaries with the prescript, "Lord of Kaga."

梅ばちの大挑灯やかすみから
ume bachi no daichōchin ya kasumi kara
(87.7)

great lanterns
with the plum blossom crest . . .
out of the mist

Sometimes the poor poet actually finds himself in the superior position vis-à-vis a daimyo, as in the following pair of haiku in which Issa contrasts favorably with a rich, but wet, provincial lord.

大名は濡れて通るを炬燵哉
daimyō wa nurete tōru wo kotatsu kana
(702.22)

a great lord
drenching wet, passes
my cozy brazier

づぶ濡[れ]の大名を見る炬燵哉
zubunu[re] no daimyō wo miru kotatsu kana
(703.5)

watching a great lord
drenched . . .
my cozy brazier

Worldly wealth and an army of samurai and
attendants cannot stop the cold winter rain. For
the moment at least, Issa, hunched over his
warm, cozy fire; seems better off than the provincial lord. Another haiku gently mocks the latter.

後供はかすみ引けり加賀の守
atodomo wa kasumi hiki keri kaga no kami
(88.8)

his attendants behind
haul the mist . . .
Lord Kaga

In Tokugawa Japan, the Shogun kept control of
the nation's daimyo by forcing them to maintain
households in Edo, thus depleting their funds
and keeping them under his watchful eye. Annu-
ally, each daimyo would travel from his province
to Edo, Edo to his province, bringing with him a
long procession of porters carrying his belong-
ings. In the haiku, Maeda, Lord of Kaga, passes
by on such a journey, followed by minions who
seem to be hauling even the mist, as if it, too, is
one of their lord's possessions. This odd image of
servants loaded down with mist gently satirizes
the daimyo's appetite to possess the world.

In another haiku about Shinano's daimyo,
Issa writes,

加賀どのの御先をついと雉哉
kaga dono no osaki wo tsui to kigisu
kana (149.2)

an impromptu audience
with Lord Kaga . . .
a pheasant.

The brash bird strolls into the Lord of Kaga's
presence without fear or concern for feudal status, suggesting that Nature cares nothing for
human hierarchy or human protocol. The socially
oblivious bird, strutting where it wants to strut,
just being itself without putting on airs; can be
viewed as "Chief Beggar" Issa himself: uninterest-
ed in, and unimpressed by, worldly power.

In Ninth Month 1817 Issa complains about a
chrysanthemum contest in which a daimyo's
flower has won first prize.

負てから大名の菊としられけり
makete kara daimyō no kiku to shirare keri
(558.18)

losing the contest
I discover
the lord's mum won

大名を味方にもつやきくの花
daimyō wo mikata ni motsu ya kiku no hana
(558.11)

the great lord
has pull . . .
chrysanthemum contest

Even in the world of flowers, there are aristocrats and peasants. Issa's flower, one of the latter, of course loses to the daimyo's blue-blooded chrysanthemum. In the second haiku, he notes, dryly, that the daimyo has "pull"—literally, "allies" (*mikata*). The world is not fair, and yet, in his art, Issa scores an ultimate victory. His poems confront the reader with an absurdity: flowers having human social status and being judged as such. This comic situation, like so many others in Issa's haiku, has satirical bite: the "great lord" appears ridiculous as he presses his influence to win a flower war.

Because he pokes fun at feudal lords in his haiku, Issa gained a reputation in Japan as a fearless iconoclast. In his 1949 study, Fujimoto Jitsuwa recounts an anecdote that illustrates Issa's "frank, unaffected manners" in the presence of worldly power (295). Although apocryphal, the story demonstrates how the poet came to be viewed by his countrymen in the years after his death. One day, Fujimoto writes, the daimyo Maeda, Lord of Kaga, was staying at Kashiwabara's inn. Hearing of Issa's fame as a haiku master, he sent for him. The village headman hurried to Issa's house, where he gushed with breathless excitement that the daimyo had summoned him to come and speak on the topic of haiku. However, to the headman's consternation, Issa responded coldly, saying, "Literary elegance doesn't follow official orders. If a noble person thinks that it does, then there's no need for us to meet" (295). The flustered headman then assured Issa that it had been a request, not an order, and so persuaded him to come to the inn.

When Issa and the Lord of Kaga finally met face to face, the anecdote continues, the former was asked to speak on the essence of his art. His response was blunt.

> The way of haiku and the way of Confucius and Buddha are the same in that if one forgets the true meaning of underlying principles and learns, in vain, only the form, he or she is a traitor. Today's haiku poets who only capture haiku's outer form, if they would observe the art's true meaning, besides the flowers, birds, wind, and moon; they would discover that all natural things under heaven that occur before their eyes or are felt in their heart can become subjects for haiku. Nevertheless, in the world there are many people who wish to devote their hearts to literary elegance but only end up clinging to outer appearances alone in their poems. Above all, it is difficult to untie the true essence of haiku for noblemen who are ignorant about the condition of common people and who wish merely to trifle with literary style. (Fujimoto 295-96)

Though clearly a fabrication, this story records a common perception of Issa in Japan: a man for whom a daimyo's pomp and circumstance meant nothing.[23]

Issa satirizes worldly authority in haiku, but he is no Edo-period revolutionary, at least not in the political sense. This is evident in his eye-witness description of a peasant's uprising at Zenkōji Town on the 13th day of Tenth Month, 1813. That year's rice crop had failed and the price of rice shot sky-high, leading to civil unrest, but Issa makes no mention of these facts. Instead, he writes that a mob of "night thieves" armed with spears and hatchets ran amok throughout the town, ransacking houses of the rich (5.130). Though he was perfectly aware of the real cause of the incident, he imputes it vaguely to an evil influence in the world: the work the Devil (maō: 魔王), and caps his comments with a haiku.

> とく暮よことしのやうな悪どしは
> *toku kure yo kotoshi no yōna akudoshi wa*
> (615.25)

> end quickly!
> this year, you've been
> an evil one

It would have been dangerous to commit to writing an encouraging or sympathetic word about a peasant insurrection. Nevertheless, Issa's moralistic take on the Zenkōji revolt resonates perfectly with his Buddhist appreciation of worldly corruption. Evil rampages through the world, but its answer can never be more evil. Issa's revolution calls for inner, spiritual change: foregoing calculated action, one simply opens heart and mind to whatever is, which brings us to the topic of "flower power."

Nature's gifts can redeem, if only for a moment, the fallen world of *mappō* and so offer a glimpse into a purity unsullied by human covetousness. This is why Issa's mood is upbeat even in "this corrupt world" (*shaba:* 娑婆) on New Year's Day, the beginning of spring in the old lunar calendar.

ことしから丸もふけ也娑婆の空

kotoshi kara marumōke nari shaba no sora
(24.18)

from this year on
clear profit . . .
this corrupt world's sky

ことしから丸儲ぞよ娑婆遊び

kotoshi kara marumōke zoyo shaba asobi
(25.1)

from this year on
clear profit, carousing
in this fallen world[24]

ことしからまふけ遊びぞ花の娑婆

kotoshi kara mōke asobi zo hana no shaba
(25.2)

from this year on
just carousing . . .
this corrupt world's blossoms

The poet rejoices despite the worldly depravity that surrounds him. In the first example, written in 1820, he seems especially optimistic as he gazes at the sky and declares that whatever time he has remaining to live in the world will be "clear profit" (*marumōke*). The following year, he expresses this idea again, pledging in our second example to devote the "clear profit" of his remaining time to "carousing." This particular haiku has a long, exultant prescript in the journal, in which Issa writes, "This first month, first day . . . the sun rising over eastern mountains, showing polished jewels of spring to greet me, my life is renewed, born again; I start fresh, walking through this world" (4.151). Strangely, the world in the Latter Days of Dharma energizes rather than depresses him, but why? The answer is suggested in our third example, another haiku of 1821, where he reveals exactly what gives him pleasure amid corruption: the blossoms of spring. New Year's Day, the first day of spring, ushers in the flowers, the haiku poet's *raison d'être*, giving him cause enough to enjoy and carouse despite the fallen age.

In one verse, a butterfly also carouses in the world of *mappō*.

蝶とぶや此世に望みないやうに
chō tobu ya kono yo ni nozomi nai yō ni
(167.17)

a butterfly flits
as if wanting nothing
in this world

The butterfly desires nothing from the world. In his translation, Blyth presents it flitting along "As if it despair[s]/ Of this world." He comments, "Our souls flutter with the inadequate wings of the butterfly, pilgrims and strangers in a world that was not made for us" (*Haiku* 2.549). Blyth's interpretation might be a bit too glum. In light of Issa's New Year's poems on this same theme, it seems more likely that the butterfly is *celebrating* life in the corrupt world. With its purity and innocence, it craves nothing in or from such a world and so is exempt from its karmic penalties; it flits through it but is not *of* it. Its wings, though fragile, are not "inadequate."[25]

In Buddhist terms, Issa's butterfly presents the possibility of detachment from the world and worldly addictions. In many of his haiku, Nature performs a parallel salvational role to that of Amida Buddha, providing people with release, though perhaps only momentary, from suffering. For example, a cool breeze in summer compensates for the poverty, misery, and oppression that humans at the bottom of the social pyramid must endure.

下々も下々下々の下国の涼しさよ
gege mo gege gege no gegoku no suzushisa yo (254.5)

it's a down, down
downtrodden land . . .
but cool!

Issa's province of Shinano is poor and downtrodden, but all who toil in its mountain-hugging fields find themselves rich with a wondrous, high-country coolness. The fallen age of *mappō* provides a broad framework for Issa's vision of society in haiku, but this framework does not entirely mold that vision. To put it another way: one might expect dreary pessimism from a poet who accepts as a religious premise the moral depravity of the ten thousand year era in which he lives, yet this is not the case with Issa. Working against the grain of cosmic *mappō*, he most typically displays spiritual optimism, lampooning secular conditions and hinting of Nature's ability, despite corruption, to provide glimpses into Buddha's Pure Land here and now.

涼しさや極楽浄土の這入口
suzushisa ya goraku jōdo no hairi-guchi
(256.10)

summer cool—
the gate to Buddha's
Pure Land

涼しさの家や浄土の西の門
suzushisa no ie ya jōdo no nishi no kado
(256.18)

a cool house—
the Pure Land's
west gate

涼風の窓が極楽浄土哉
suzukaze no mado ga gokuraku jōdo kana
(256.24)

cool breeze
through the window . . .
Pure Land Paradise!

It is as if the Pure Land has palpably invaded the world, rescuing its inhabitants from summer's heat. These poems can be viewed as merely metaphorical; Issa simply conveys his appreciation for the coolness by means of exaggerated, paradisiacal imagery. Perhaps, however, he is not using metaphor or exaggerating at all: the summer coolness *is* the gate to Buddha's Pure Land, which situates the Western Paradise not very far from this world. In fact, it is so near, Issa suggests, its perfect air spills easily into our corrupt world of *mappō*, now and then—if one is open to it.

In similar fashion, spring's cherry blossoms usher a divine splendor into the everyday world.

天からでも降たるやうに桜哉

ten kara de mo futtaru yō ni sakura kana
(228.8)

like they fell
from heaven . . .
cherry blossoms

夜ざくらや美人天から下るとも

yozakura ya bijin ten kara kudaru tomo
(233.11)

night's cherry blossoms—
heavenly ladies
among us

The first haiku is a favorite of Issa's, appearing in six different texts. In it, he makes use of a simile: the cherry blossoms look "like they fell/ from heaven." The second haiku is an even stronger statement, wherein the blossoms appear as heavenly "ladies" (*bijin*), a touch of poetic fancy that emphasizes how exquisite, delicate, feminine, and precious they are. As in the cool breeze/Pure land examples, Issa again *might* be using metaphor— but, also again, a literal reading is possible and, I believe, preferable. The beautiful blossoms are, *in fact*, a heavenly gift. Paradise invades the world of suffering and so relieves its sufferers, here and now. This "heaven" with its courtly ladies is the mythic palace of Chinese tradition, not Amida's Western Paradise. Nevertheless, Issa's point is consistent. Coolness wafts eastward into the world from the Pure Land; cherry blossoms fill it as if denizens of Heaven's court. In both cases, Nature's gifts transform the universe, just as Amida Buddha's saving grace transforms those who trust in it.

The notion that spring's blossoms can temporarily remedy the corruption of the age of *mappō* is so common in Issa that examples are legion. Here are three more.

花咲や欲のうきよの片すみに

hana saku ya yoku no ukiyo no kata sumi ni
(211.12)

blossoms bloom—
in a nook in this floating
world of craving

此やうな末世を桜だらけ哉

kono yōna masse wo sakura darake kana
(229.6)

this fallen world
plastered
with cherry blossoms

元日やどちらむいても花の娑婆

ganjitsu ya dochira muite mo hana no shaba
(23.21)

New Year's Day—
in every direction, the corrupt
world's blossoms

Like summer's coolness and spring's cherry blossoms, the nightingale's song—another springtime gift—manifests such stunning purity that Issa feels that it *must* originate in Paradise.

鶯や弥陀の浄土の東門

uguisu ya mida no jōdo no higashi kado
(137.1)

a nightingale sings—
the Pure Land's
east gate

And in this widely cited and translated example, heavenly birdsong is equated with Buddhist scripture.

今の世も鳥はほけ経鳴にけり

ima no yo mo tori wa hokekyō naki ni keri
(136.4)

the world today—
a bird sings
the Lotus Sutra[26]

This poem was composed in Second Month, 1819, with the prescript, "Heavenly Music," in *Hachiban nikki* (4.39). The bird's heavenly rendition of the Lotus Sutra contrasts ironically with the "the world today" (*ima no yo*), a stock phrase that denotes the latter days of *mappō* in which the divine song of the bird sounds all that more miraculous or, depending on one's point of view, out of place. Issa liked this haiku enough to include it in *Oraga haru*. In the long passage that introduces it in that text, he reports that people in the area claimed to have heard "heavenly music" on New Year's Day and every eighth day thereafter (6.138). Although local skeptics dismissed the phenomenon as merely the sound of blowing wind, Issa seems to have taken it seriously. Perhaps, he writes, heavenly music was indeed trickling into the world, and those who did not hear it were prevented by the limitations of their own "sinful lives" (6.138). He and some colleagues stayed up all night on the 19th day of Third Month, listening. They heard nothing until dawn, at which time the single voice of a bird broke the silence. Significantly, the "divine music" came not from beyond the fallen world but from *within* it. Once again, Issa expresses the idea that Paradise is palpably present when one opens one's heart to Nature, looking and listening. Appraised in this way, this world *is* the Pure Land.

In Issa's poetic vision, the corrupt and corrupting age of *mappō* finds remedy in the power of Nature. Under the spring blossoms and autumn moon, bickering ceases and class differences subside.

花の陰赤の他人はなかりけり

hana no kage aka no tanin wa nakari keri
(216.11)

in cherry blossom shade
no one
is a stranger

名月や出家士諸商人

meigetsu ya shukke samurai shoakindo
(459.25)

harvest moon-gazing
priests, samurai,
merchants

The first haiku is difficult to translate. As Henderson points out, it is structured in the original Japanese so that it ends with a revelation (130): "In blossom shade, as for complete strangers, they exist . . . not!" The fact that the negation comes last puts emphasis on how the blossoms have countermanded ordinary reality—a reality in which people *are*, normally, strangers to one another. The cherry blossoms nevertheless draw them together and, for a moment at least, make them one.[27] In similar fashion, people of different social classes—priests, samurai, and merchants—unite under the harvest moon in the second haiku, its divine light making them all forget, at least for now, divisions, prejudices, and jealousies. Such moments of epiphany, when one opens heart and mind to Nature's gifts of spring blossoms and autumn moon, make the suffering world in the Latter Days of Dharma seem . . . like Paradise.

Chapter 4. *MUJŌ:* Transience

These two haiku appear back-to-back in Issa's journal, *Shichiban nikki* in Sixth Month, 1815.

魚どもは桶としらでや夕涼
uo domo wa oke to shirade ya yūsuzumi
(322.5)

fish
unaware of the bucket . . .
a cool evening

庖丁で鰻よりつつ夕すずみ
hōchō de unagi yoritsutsu yūsuzumi (322.11)

with a kitchen knife
choosing eels . . .
a cool evening

The fish in the first poem are blissfully ignorant of irony, of the bucket, and of what that bucket means for their future. Instead of fretting about becoming someone's dinner, they swim in the present moment, circling in the cool water. In the second example, a cook's knife plucks out specimens of roiling, slippery life. While Issa may sympathize with the eels, his tone is not tragic. Choosing eels to be eaten is simply part of the scene, like the cool evening air that the cook, the poet, and even, perhaps, the eels themselves are enjoying . . . for the moment. But this moment of happiness will not last for any of the parties involved.[28]

A basic tenet of all forms of Buddhism is "the truth that life involves impermanence and constant change" (Ross 36). One of Issa's nineteenth century commentators, Seian Saiba, singles out impermanence (*mujō*: 無常) as a prevalent theme in his haiku (Kobayashi Issa 6.165). Indeed, Issa's diaries are chock-full of verses about dissolving dewdrops, scattering blossoms, falling leaves, melting snow, and other natural manifestations of transience. Implicit in such imagery is a sense of the poet's own mortality. These two haiku of 1810 appear back-to-back in *Shichiban nikki* (3.38).

さく花に長逗留の此世哉
saku hana ni naga-tōryū no kono yo kana
(210.29)

among blooming flowers—
a long stay
in this world

さく花や此世住居も今少[し]
*saku hana ya kono yo zumai mo ima
suko[shi]* (211.3)

blooming flowers—
residents of this world, too,
for a short time

Compared to the blossoms that live and die in a season, the 48-year-old poet feels ancient. Yet in the very next haiku of the diary he identifies with the flowers, sensing that his own stay in the world will be brief, too.

The tolling of temple bells often reminds Issa of the inevitable.

身の上の鐘としりつつ夕がすみ

mi no ue no kane to shiritsutsu yūgasumi
(88.12)

knowing the bell
rings away life . . .
evening mist

身の上の鐘と知りつつ夕涼み

mi no ue no kane to shiritsutsu yūsuzumi
(320.9)

knowing the bell
rings away life . . .
evening cool

In a revision of the second haiku, the listener is oblivious to the bell's cosmic message.

身の上の鐘ともしらで夕涼み

mi no ue no kane tomo shirade yūsuzumi
(320.9, variant)

not knowing the bell
rings away life . . .
evening cool

In the first two haiku, "for whom the bell tolls" is fully understood; in the third, it is not. Issa implies that awareness of transience may be irrelevant. Whether one realizes it or not, time passes and life slips away. He advises even flies and worms to heed the bell's warning.

無常鐘蝿虫めらもよっくきけ

mujō-gane hae mushimera mo yokku kike
(376.20)

the bell of life passing—
O flies and worms
listen well![29]

The notion of philosophical insects and worms contemplating the cosmic meaning a temple bell is a silly bit of haiku humor, yet a serious truth is expressed in the poem and reaches, if not the crawlers and squirmers, Issa's human audience: life is short, and, always, shorter than one thinks.

Issa does not invoke the theme of transience merely as a centuries-old cliché of Japanese poetry. Throughout his work his treatment of *mujō* reveals a profound and discerning grasp of the concept in relation to Buddhist tradition. A prime example is the following.

時鳥火宅の人を笑らん

hototogisu kataku no hito wo warauran
(337.12)

cuckoo—
laughing at the man
in the burning house?

The burning house is an allusion to the Lotus Sutra, Chapter 3. In this particular passage the Universal Buddha instructs his disciples that there is but one path to salvation, not the three paths that tradition has established. He explains this truth by means of a parable about a man who owns a huge, crumbling mansion that catches fire. The man's three children, "addicted . . . to their pleasures," remain inside the house, happily playing games (Hurvitz 69). Unconcerned about the flames and malignant beasts that surround them, the children continue playing, even though their father is shouting for them to come outside. In their innocence, they cannot understand words such as "perish" or "fire." Finally, the father strikes upon a clever ruse: he promises each child a bright new carriage. Lured by this promise of playthings, they leave the doomed mansion just in time.

The Buddha goes on to interpret his allegory. The man in the story, he explains, is himself, "the Father of the world," and the three children are living beings, addicted to "worldly pleasure" (72). The carriages represent the three traditional schools of Buddhism that in fact are merely expedients to attain a single goal: to lure sentient beings out of the firetrap of desire, their fatal attachment to things in this impermanent universe of "sickness, death, and care" (72). In Issa's haiku, a cuckoo seems to be laughing at a person trapped by flames of destruction. On one level, the poet is surely poking fun at himself, but Issa is not only the man in the burning house; he is also the singing cuckoo outside. His poetic vision embraces both perspectives. Unlike fish circling in a cook's tub or those listeners who fail to understand what the evening bell is telling them, Issa is fully aware of mortality and fleeting time. He is trapped in a house on fire, yet, in his mind, he is free, laughing at his cosmic predicament in the guise of a cuckoo.

Kenkō, an essayist of the late thirteenth and early fourteenth centuries, notes, "If man were never to fade away like the dews of Adashino, never to vanish like the smoke over Toribeyama, but lingered on forever in the world, how things would lose their power to move us" (7)! Cherry blossoms and dewy fields move us precisely because, so soon, blossoms scatter and dew burns away. Issa also recognizes this hidden benefit of *mujō*.

仏法がなくば光らじ草の露
buppō ga nakuba hikaraji kusa no tsuyu
(480.15)

without Buddha's law
no glitter . . .
dewdrops in the grass

Buppō, translated here as "Buddha's law," denotes dharma. Derived from the Sanskrit word, *darmah* ("law"), dharma is not only the principle of righteousness but also the supreme truth that the universe embodies. The Burmese monk U Thittila explains: "*Dhamma* [dharma] is the true nature of every existing thing, animate and inanimate. If a man will live by *Dhamma*, he will escape misery and come to *Nibbana* [nirvana], the final release from all suffering" (Ross 95). The dewdrops shine brightly thanks to Buddha's law of transience; their sparkle is precious precisely to the extent that it is brief.

The path to Buddhist "release from all suffering" can be found in ephemeral dewdrops, provided that one knows how to read them.

露ちるや後生大事に鳴雀

tsuyu chiru ya goshō daiji ni naku suzume
(475.29)

dewdrops scatter—
the sparrow sings
of next-life salvation

朝露に浄土参りのけいこ哉

asa tsuyu ni jōdo mairi no keiko kana
(477.12)

the morning dew
teaches the way . . .
to the Pure Land

只頼め頼めと露のこぼれけり

tada tanome tanome to tsuyu no kobore keri
(478.8)

"Simply trust! trust!"
dewdrops spilling
down

The sparrow "preaches" amid the glistening dewdrops that embody the text of its sermon. Similarly, in the second example the morning dew is a Pure Land "lesson" (*keiko*). What is implied in the first two haiku is stated overtly in the third: since everything in the world is temporary, one must cling not to worldly things but to Amida Buddha's vow. The way to the Pure Land is the dewdrop way, spilling to oblivion while faithfully trusting in the Buddha.

In this previously cited haiku, dewdrops quarrel with the dharma-law of the universe.

露ちるやむさい此世に用なしと

tsuyu chiru ya musai kono yo ni yō nashi to
(477.21)

dewdrops scatter—
"Goodbye, cruel
world!"

Issa leaves the reader to imagine whether the haiku is the lament of a single dewdrop or many. Either way, the dew in question bids good riddance to the foul world of corruption and sorrow. Yet, like the cuckoo laughing at the man in the burning house, Issa seems to be chuckling at these overly melodramatic drops—and, indirectly, at humans who manifest such an attitude. To struggle against the nature of things, to die complaining about the world rather than trusting in something beyond it, is a grave error . . .

And *yet!* In Issa's most famous haiku on transience, a poem of grieving for a dead daughter, Buddhist teaching seems to fail him.

露の世は露の世ながらさりながら

tsuyu no yo wa tsuyu no yo nagara sari nagara (480.23)

this world
is a dewdrop world
yes . . . but . . .

The French translator, Collet, uses the ending of this haiku (*nagara sari nagara*: "and yet, and yet") for the title of his 1991 book, *Issa: et pourtant, et pourtant* ("Issa: And yet, and yet"). For Collet and for many readers, this poignant verse is Issa's signature poem. Written in honor of little Sato, it is a revision of an earlier haiku that commemorates the one-year anniversary of the death of Sentarō, Issa's first child. This original version is prefaced with the single word, "Grieving."

露の世は得心ながらさりながら

tsuyu no yo wa tokushin nagara sari nagara
(480.1)

it's a dewdrop world
surely it is
yes . . . but . . .

Buddhism recommends detachment from all fleeting persons and things inside this "dewdrop world," *and yet* the poet cannot accept the loss of his darling children with philosophical detachment. It may be true that all things pass, but Issa adds, and one can almost hear his voice drop to a bare whisper, "yes . . . but . . . "

In a lighter, more typical mood, Issa (or someone) expedites a dewdrop's fade to oblivion.

露の玉つまんだ時も仏哉

tsuyu no tama tsumanda toki mo hotoke
kana (480.20)

a dewdrop pearl—
I pinched it into
a Buddha

The "I" could just as well be translated "he" or
"she." The point is: someone has pinched a little
ball of morning dew, hastening it to become "a
Buddha," a polite way of saying it is dead. There
is, however, deeper implication in this little
comedy. Once pinched, the dewdrop is perfectly
nothing: a void that does not strive, desire, calculate, or cling to the self that is no longer there
(and never really existed in the first place). It has
gained release from the world of suffering—just
like Buddha.

This next haiku of transience was composed
in the final year of Issa's own dewdrop life.

一つきへ二つきへつつ灯籠哉

hitotsu kie futatsu kie-tsutsu tōro kana
(494.12)

one dies out
two die out . . .
lanterns for the dead

The scene is a cemetery at the time of the autumn
Bon Festival grave visits. Family members have lit
lanterns for their dear departed ones, but these
lanterns, as they die out, embody the truth of the

impermanence that governs the world and has filled so many graves. The flames succumb to darkness, one by one, while Issa watches . . . and counts.

In his commentary on *Oraga haru*, Seian Saiba seems correct in claiming that Issa teaches Buddhist transience through his poetry. However, these lessons are not simplistic, superficial, or dogmatic. Issa explores dharma from myriad angles, including the most personal and most human. In one moment his stay in the world seems brief—an orthodox statement—yet in another he marvels at how amazingly long it has been. The temple bell "rings away life," yet this fact does not detract from the haunting beauty of an evening mist or the refreshing coolness of the evening air. The fish enjoying the cool water of their bucket seem tragically unaware of how the universe works, and yet, Issa hints, perhaps they are wise to live fully, energetically in the present. The same goes for flies and worms; Issa urges them to "listen well" to the tolling bell of life passing, but this advice, couched in archaic literary language, makes the poet seem the misguided one, absurdly out of touch with the natural way of things, which it to embrace, utterly, the now. Issa's haiku of impermanence express contradictory ideas, for such is the complexity of the subject. He is the man in the burning house of desire, and yet he is also the cuckoo outside, free and laughing. In some haiku moments, *mujō* seems a lucky thing, for it endows the world with fragile beauty and teaches one to surrender trustingly to Amida Buddha. *And yet*, in other moments of mourning and loss Buddhist admonitions about living in a "dewdrop world" sound hollow.

Whether lucky or tragic, transience is inevitable . . . and natural.

はらはらと畠のこやしや桜花

hara-hara to hata no koyashi ya sakura kana
(232.8)

fluttering down
mulch for the field . . .
cherry blossoms

The blossoms' death is necessary in the cycle of life, for they add to the mulch upon which future blossoms will one day thrive. Acceptance of this fact explains the odd tranquility of this next poem.

ちる花にあごを並べる蛙哉

chiru hana ni ago wo naraberu kawazu kana
(159.19)

chin-deep
in the fallen blossoms . . .
frog!

Like the frog, we find ourselves chin-deep in a world that owes much of its beauty to the fact that nothing in it will last.

When he returned to Kashiwabara after years of restless traveling (Eleventh Month, 1812), Issa composed a haiku of transience that his disciples would later come to view as his death verse, etching it on his gravestone.

是がまあつひの栖か雪五尺
kore ga maa tsui no sumika ka yuki go shaku
(641.32)

well here it is,
my final home?
five feet of snow

Issa's "final home" (*tsui no sumika*) lies buried under five feet of snow, not unusual for Kashiwabara in wintertime. When he wrote this, he hadn't yet resolved his inheritance dispute and so was staying in a rented house in the village: back in his hometown but not quite home. The outcome of the family struggle was still in doubt, so the question, "my final home?" reflects genuine uncertainty. In a later, undated revision he changes the middle phrase to pose a slightly different, though just as biographically grounded, question: "Is this, then, my death place?" (*shinidokoro ka yo*; 641.32, variant). In both versions, Issa wonders if he is home for good. Snow covers the village, suggesting the coldness of a homecoming to a place with no loved ones to welcome him. At age fifty-two, entering the winter of his life, he has returned to Kashiwabara with enough time remaining, he muses, only to prepare for the grave—a striking invocation of *mujō* in a haiku that is both intimately personal and universally evocative.

He moved permanently into his side of the divided farmhouse in autumn of 1813 and, the following spring, got married. He was fifty-two by

Japanese reckoning; his bride, Kiku, twenty-eight. On their wedding day, the 11th day of Fourth Month, he records in his diary, succinctly, "Clear weather. The wife came" (3.305). That same year, in Ninth Month, he writes a poem that, as Collet points out (13), might be a playful allusion to his late-in-life marriage.

人ならば五十位ぞ鹿の恋
hito naraba go jū kurai zo shika no koi
(521.25)

if you were human
you could be about fifty . . .
mating deer

Issa had finally married, but it had taken him over fifty years, which left precious little time for domestic bliss. Any young deer cavorting on a wooded mountain seems luckier than such a groom.

After Issa and Kiku wed, the next order of business was making children. Kiku gave birth to the couple's first son, Sentarō, on the 14th day of Fourth Month, 1816, according to Issa's diary (3.419). However, in Fifth Month Sentarō, twenty-seven days old, died. According to Yoshida Miwako, the following haiku, written two months later, alludes to Issa's family struggling to bloom (202).

夕顔の次其次が我家かな
yūgao no tsugi sono tsugi ga waga ya kana
(391.19)

after the moonflowers
blooming even later . . .
my house

In Fifth Month of 1818, Kiku gave birth to a daughter, Sato, but, sadly, history repeated itself; the next year the baby caught smallpox and died. Issa writes in *Oraga haru* a long, heartfelt prose description of her passing, which concludes,

> In the end, on the 21st day of Sixth Month, together with the morning-glory blossoms, she withered. Her mother clinging to the corpse, burst into tears. At this moment, although I tried to resign myself to the fact that water, once it flows past, doesn't come by a second time, or blossoms, once fallen, never return to the trees . . . I couldn't break the chain of love. (6.150)

After the funeral, on the occasion of burying Sato's ashes, Issa revises his earlier haiku of mourning, creating a poem that, we have noted, many regard as his signature piece.

露の世は露の世ながらさりながら
tsuyu no yo wa tsuyu no yo nagara sari nagara (480.23)

this world
is a dewdrop world
yes . . . but . . .

In another text, he copies this verse and adds the prescript, "On losing a beloved child" (1.480).

In autumn 1820 a boy, Ishitarō, was born, but once again the Buddhist truth of *mujō* had personal, gut-wrenching consequences. Shortly after New Year's 1821, this third child died of suffocation while bundled on his mother's back. Issa mourned.

陽炎や目につきまとふ笑い顔
kagerō ya me ni tsukimatō warai-gao (93.4)

heat shimmers—
his smiling face
lingers

なで[し]こののなぜ折たぞよおれたぞよ
nade[shi]ko no naze oreta zoyo oreta zoyo (401.4)

why did the blooming
pink break?
oh why?

These haiku appear back-to-back in *Hachiban nikki* as First Month entries for 1821. In the same journal Issa records Ishitarō's death with characteristic terseness: "Eleventh Day, Ishitarō, dead" (4. 153). Later that year, he writes wistfully about this third lost child.

石太郎此世にあらば盆踊
ishitarō kono yo ni araba bon odori (496.31)

if Ishitarō
were still in this world . . .
Bon Festival dance

In another haiku of 1821, he might be alluding to his own life and losses.

あきらめて子のない鹿は鳴ぬなり
akiramete ko no nai shika wa nakinu nari
(523.9)

giving up
the childless deer
calls no more for love

The deer, a buck, doesn't bother with a mating call, just as the childless poet, for the moment at least, seems to have given up hope of progeny. A haiku written a month later refers to the domestic situation.

春待や子のない家ももちをつく
haru matsu ya ko no nai ie mo mochi wo tsuku (675.9)

waiting for spring
in a house without children
pounding rice cakes

Issa and Kiku tried once more. In 1822, Third Month, a male child, Konzaburō, was born—only to outlive his mother. She fell ill and died in spring, 1823. Issa writes with an almost audible sigh.

小言いふ相手もあらばけふの月
kogoto iu aite mo araba kyō no tsuki (460.16)

if only she were here
for me to nag . . .
tonight's moon!

In the first edition of this book I rendered the phrase, *kogoto iu aite*, as "my nagging companion," but Shinji Ōgawa has since explained that, grammatically, it is Issa, not Kiku, who nagged. This doesn't necessarily contradict the prescript that Issa later adds to this haiku in one text: "My fault-finding old wife passed away this year" (1.460). Shinji notes that "my nagging old wife" is simply a typical public statement of humility. In light of Shinji's clarification, I owe an apology to Lewis Mackenzie and Sam Hamill for stating in my essay, "Translating Translations: A Disturbing Trend," that they mistranslated this haiku when they depicted Issa, not his wife, as the grumbler. However, since Mackenzie and Hamill are right, Lucien Stryk must be wrong (as I was) when he renders the first phrase of the haiku, "my bitter wife" (94). When Issa remembers his nagging of Kiku, his tone is one of fond and wistful longing, as in the following poem.

小言いふ相手もあらば菊の酒
kogoto iu aite mo araba kiku no sake (504.19)

if only she were here
for me to nag . . .
mum festival sake

The autumn mum festival evokes the memory of his own lost mum blossom, for this is the meaning of Kiku in Japanese. In 1823, the fourth child, Kinsarō, joined his siblings and mother in the pine-shaded graveyard.

In 1824 Issa remarried . . . briefly. The wedding took place in Fifth Month, the divorce in Eighth Month. His new bride, twenty-eight year-old Yuki, was the daughter of a local samurai. Her name, "Snow," fit her well, for she quickly turned a cold shoulder to the slovenly, "just as I am" poet and fled to her parents' home. Issa gives no indication in the diaries that he missed her. Instead, a month after the divorce, he writes again, longingly, of his first wife.

小言いふ相手もあらば花莚

kogoto iu aite mo araba hana mushiro (220.8)

if only my nagging
companion were here . . .
blossom viewing mat

Only one haiku, undated, makes reference to his ephemeral second marriage; it has the prescript, "Divorce."

へちまづる切って支舞ば他人哉

hechima-zuru kitte shimaeba tanin kana
(594.8)

after cutting
the snake gourd vine . . .
strangers[30]

As easily and as irrevocably as snipping a garden vine, Issa found himself alone again, a "stranger" (*tanin*) to wife number two.

He tried one last time to make a family. In 1826 he married again, this time to a thirty-two year-old local woman named Yao. She right away gave birth to a daughter, Yata, the only one of the poet's children who would survive to adulthood. Sadly, Issa never met her. The pregnancy began in the Tenth Year of Bunsei, 1827: a hard time during which Issa's divided house burned down in a village fire and the couple moved into a grain barn on the property. The poet died of a stroke that winter, on the 19th day of Eleventh Month. Yata was born five months later. The Buddhist theme of life and loving attachments dissolving to oblivion was no mere intellectual concept for Kobayashi Issa but rather the day-to-day reality that more than anything else defined his latter years.

A discussion of Issa's dewdrop life would not be complete without mentioning two poems, each of which different commentators have claimed to be his last.

盥から盥にうつるちんぷんかん (Mackenzie 46)
tarai kara tarai ni utsuru chimpunkan

moving
from tub to tub . . .
empty babble

ありがたや衾の雪も浄土より (Mackenzie 46)
arigata ya fusuma no yuki mo jōdo yori

grateful—
the snow on my quilt
from the Pure Land!

Texts of these haiku do not exist in Issa's hand, and so they are considered to be apocryphal; Kobayashi Keiichirō and the other editors of *Issa zenshū* leave them out of their authoritative collection. However, some translators of haiku into Western languages continue to present them as if they are Issa's work.[31] Issa didn't seem to write them, but the "tub-to-tub" and the "snow on my quilt" poems have been linked to him by posterity, possibly thanks to admiring disciples who felt the need for a "last word" from the master. The first haiku is a witty summation of life worthy of Issa; from the tub used to wash the newborn child to the tub for bathing the corpse, it all adds up to *chimpunkan*: nonsense, mumbo jumbo, empty babble. The second haiku, also very much in Issa's style, refers to the Pure Land leaking into the present world, a favorite theme of the poet that we noted in the previous chapter. Whoever composed these death poems, they certainly reveal what contemporaries perceived to be essential in Issa: ironic wit, deeply religious sentiment, and, permeating all, a feeling of life's transience.

The dewdrop-like elusiveness of happiness in Issa's life, a theme that the poet himself raises in countless haiku, has led many critics to stress his human and suffering side. One of the first to take this approach was Nakamura Rikurō. His preface to his 1921 anthology, *Issa senshū*, is an early example of such criticism, though, as the following excerpts show, he does not miss the

Pure Land Buddhism that was so central to the poet's life and art—something that many later critics ignore or gloss over. In his introduction, Nakamura relates a conversation that he had, months earlier, during the course of which he was asked, "Since Haiku Master Bashō and Haiku Master Buson each have had their complete works published, why hasn't Haiku Master Issa?" (1). Nakamura reports that he answered in this way: "Issa of Haiku Temple holds a unique position in the world of haiku. As a person, as a sincere human being, there is value in studying him, yet actually very few people are undertaking such study" (1). Nakamura goes on to explain that the title of "haiku master," which applies so fittingly to Bashō and Buson, is something that Issa himself would probably have rejected: "Issa followed the salvation-by-Other-Power sect. He believed in being saved by the Buddha while behaving humanly and without effort, despite bad karma and carnal desires. He presented himself as a grateful old man who trusted fully in the power of 'Namu Amida Butsu,' and thus he would have shunned the title of 'master'" (4). Nakamura cites the concluding haiku of *Oraga haru*.

ともかくもあなた任せのとしの暮
tomokaku mo anata makase no toshi no kure
(616.19)

come what may
trusting in the Buddha . . .
the year ends

He comments, "Issa . . . suffered more than his share of pains and sorrows. The human misery of divorce and losing children afflicted his heart without end . . . Issa was an ordinary man who humanly suffered and humanly prayed" (5-6).

Many critics and readers, like Nakamura, have dwelled on the tragic, "human" side of Issa. In the twentieth century, books about the poet published in Japan were not considered complete if they failed to emphasize his pain and troubles: the deaths of his mother and grandmother in his childhood, his cruel treatment by his stepmother, his exile to the capital, the long and bitter dispute over his inheritance, the deaths of his first wife and four infant children, the divorce of his second wife, his bouts with paralysis, and the fire that destroyed his home and left him to spend his last year in a cramped, musty grain-barn—a structure that still stands today in Kashiwabara village. This approach misses the fact that most of his haiku are joyful celebrations of the universe and being alive in it. Even when he writes of *mujō* his tone is most often cheerful and accepting. In Pure Land Buddhist terms, transience is not necessarily a bad thing; it means, simply, that there is nothing permanent in the world to which one can cling, so one can only rely on Amida Buddha as the sole hope for rescue.

弥陀仏の見ておはす也ちる桜
mida butsu no mite owasu nari chiru sakura
(232.16)

Amida Buddha watches
them scatter . . .
cherry blossoms

Throughout his works, Issa's hopeful faith in Amida's compassion far outweighs the grumbling doubts of his darkest moments—as our remaining chapters will show.

Chapter 5. *JINEN:* Naturalness

Historically speaking, the first Buddha became such through an act of meditation. Siddhartha Gautama sat under a fig tree, locked his legs together in the lotus position, and waited. He vowed not to budge from the spot until he attained Supreme Enlightenment. He kept this vow. In the sixth century B.C.E., in a place in ancient India shaded by what would later be called the Bodhi Tree, the Tree of Wisdom, the man Siddhartha woke up, and Buddha was born.[32]

What he experienced on that day under that tree cannot be expressed or explained in words, according to Nancy Wilson (14). However, she does her best to *describe* the experience.

> As a term, enlightenment signifies a direct, dynamic spiritual experience brought about, in the Buddhist view, through the faculty of intuition, a faculty developed and sharpened by such spiritual disciplines as intensive meditation and contemplation. It is a condition beyond the power and pull of "the opposites," a full realization of the universe and the self as one. (15)

Unlike other figures in world religions, Wilson notes, the Buddha's enlightenment did not involve divine intervention. For Gautama Buddha, Nirvana "lay in the here-and-now [. . .] not in some remote realm or celestial state far beyond one's present existence" (16).

Seeking to duplicate his experience under the Bodhi Tree, the Buddha's followers of the Zen school adopted sitting meditation as a central practice. In sitting Zen, one keeps perfectly still, open to that which is, intuiting connection and oneness where ordinary eyes see division and separateness. The first master of haiku, Matsuo Bashō, studied Zen and imbued his own art with the sensibilities of that sect. Thanks to Bashō, the one-breath poetry of haiku came to demand of its most serious practitioners the same attitude of Gautama Buddha under the Wisdom Tree: one of openness, receptivity, and non-intellectual, intuitive insight. A frog leaps into an old pond, and the poet, attentive to the here-and-now, focuses attention on the simple "plop!" of the water (*mizu no oto*). With words Bashō intimates connections that lie beyond words; through language he arrives at pregnant silence.[33]

Issa did not belong to the Zen sect, nor is there evidence that he studied Zen or practiced sitting meditation. As a Pure Land Buddhist, he probably viewed the Zen approach as a misguided exercise of "self-power." Gautama Buddha's heroic accomplishment under the Bodhi Tree, according to Pure Land Buddhism, cannot be duplicated in this fallen and corrupt age. Now, the Other Power of Amida Buddha is one's only hope for rebirth in the Pure Land and, concomitant to that, enlightenment. Yet, despite his Jōdoshinshū orientation, Issa's haiku reflect many of the values of contemplative Buddhism, since haiku art generally, and that of his master Chikua's school in particular, were to a large degree shaped by Bashō. As Blyth points out, the "Zen state of mind" was central to the haiku of Bashō and those who emulated him (*Haiku* 1.16; cf. 23-39; 154-238).

However he came to it, Issa learned to practice and portray a patient openness to the here-and-now.

大仏の鼻から出たる乙鳥哉

daibutsu no hana kara detaru tsubame kana
(141.20)

from the great bronze
Buddha's nose . . .
a swallow!

The haiku ends with *kana*, a particle of emphasis that conveys a sense of "Ah! Imagine that!" In the present case, the immense statue sneezes a swallow from its cavernous nostril, or, as Bob Jones envisions the moment, a whole flock of them "pour forth" (49). Either way, Issa gasps with delight as the Great Buddha—ponderous, motionless, vast—breathes out the quick, darting bird(s).

In haiku after haiku, this pattern of quiet observance followed by stunning revelation is repeated, and in this way Issa's poetic method recapitulates the sitting and awakening of Buddha under the Bodhi Tree. Though he makes no claim or even suggests that nirvana waits at the end of his one-breath poems, Issa typically concludes them with a surprise, an insight into the marvel of the ordinary—much in keeping with the spirit of Buddhist awakening.

ゆうぜんとして山を見る蛙哉

yūzen to shite yama wo miru kawazu kana
(159.26)

serene and still
mountain viewing
frog

This haiku appears in *Hachiban nikki* in 1813 without comment, but Issa recopies it six years later in *Oraga haru* with a prose preface: "In the summer evening, spreading my straw mat, I call 'Lucky! Lucky!' and soon he comes crawling out from his hiding place in the thicket, enjoying the evening cool just like a person" (6.143). The editors of *Issa zenshū* explain that "Lucky" (*fuku*) is a pet name for toads, suggesting that some of the "frogs" in Issa's haiku might in fact be toads (6.169, note 114). In any case, on its surface the haiku is comic. Someone is sitting "serene and still," gazing at a mountain or mountains, but in the end—the punch line—this gazing someone turns out to be . . . a frog! Deeper than its bait-and-switch humor, the haiku reveals the deep kinship of Lucky and Issa. They both enjoy the cool evening air, gaze at the mountain, and do so with an attitude of utter tranquility. Issa describes their shared experience with the word, *yūzen:* "boundless calm." Frog and poet sit in profound meditation. Lucky the Frog, like Issa, is a Buddhist.[34]

In many of Issa's haiku, an action rather than a thing reveals itself before the aftermath of silence. The following haiku, for example, ends with a verb.

牛もうもうもうと霧から出たりけり
ushi mō mō mō to kiri kara detari keri (487.12)

moo, moo, moo
from the mist cows
emerge

In his translation, Blyth imagines one cow in the scene (*Haiku* 1.10-11), but I prefer to visualize several. In either case, the climactic word, the focus of attention and delight, is *detari*, to "come forth," to "emerge." The miracle of cows in their ponderous bodies materializing from the nothingness of autumn mist is so natural, so ordinary, and yet, when one *really* looks and listens . . . so astounding.

Issa's attentiveness to the natural and ordinary has a special significance in Pure Land tradition. Shinran advises that one should practice naturalness, spontaneity, and non-striving (*jinen*) in the quest to attain enlightenment. D. T. Suzuki elaborates: "*Jinen* thus means that because one's rebirth in the Pure Land is wholly due to the working of Amida's vow-power, the devotee simply believes in Amida and lets the vow work itself out" (71). Shinran stresses non-striving throughout his writings. In one of his epistles, he coins the maxim, "In Other Power no self working is true working" (*Letters* 29). Without calculation, relying on the spontaneous workings of *jinen*, the believer emulates Nature's own non-forcing. Trusting in the saving vow of Amida Buddha, one simply lets salvation come *jinen*, "of itself." According to Bloom, Shinran's attitude of *kono mama* ("being just as I am") is a rejection of self-assertion that has its roots in Chinese Taoism (*Shinran's Gospel* 43-44).

Both in the subject matter of his haiku and in his method of composing them, Issa manifests Shinran's principle of *kono mama:* an off-the-cuff, "just as I am," naturalness. Nature, for the Buddhist, implies no outside "Doer" or "Creator." In this vein, the Japanese word for Nature, *jinen* (modern pronunciation = *shizen*) denotes spontaneity—that which is "of itself so." Emulating Nature's spontaneity in his poetic method and celebrating that spontaneity as subject matter, Issa delights in the unforced, "of-itself-ness" of things.

門口や自然生なる松の春

kado guchi ya jinen bae-naru matsu no haru
(29.1)

at my gate
wildly it grows . . .
spring pine

No one outside of the pine has planned its urgent growth; nothing outside of the pine is making it. Spontaneously, effortlessly . . . it simply *is*.[35]

Semantically related to *jinen* ("Nature"), the Japanese word *onozukara* describes an action that occurs "naturally," "spontaneously," and "of itself-ly." Issa uses this expression in several haiku, including these three.

おのづから頭の下たるぼたん哉

onozukara zu no sagaritaru botan kana
(394.25)

by itself
the head bows . . .
peony!

梅しんとしておのづから頭が下る
ume shin to shite onozukara zu ga sagaru
(203.17)

for plum blossoms
the head, by itself,
bows

おのづから頭が下る也梅の花
onozukara zu ga sagaru nari ume no hana
(204.1)

by itself
the head bows . . .
plum blossoms!

The poet's head bows without conscious
intention. The peony and plum trees that have
bloomed spontaneously are met with appropri-
ately spontaneous gestures, and Issa's act of
recording the moments is just as unforced, simple, and natural. In *Hachiban nikki*, the second
and third examples appear back-to-back (4.228).
Issa evidently preferred the first version, since he
recopied it in two other texts with prescripts that
situate the poem in Second Month during "an all-
night vigil" (1.203). Stylistically, the haiku is as
spontaneous and natural as the scene that it
evokes.

In a related verse, he finds himself bowing to a sacred hill.

おのづから頭が下る也神ぢ山
onozukara zu ga sagaru nari kamiji yama
(747.11)

by itself
the head bows . . .
Mount Kamiji

Mount Kamiji is a hill dedicated to the sun goddess Amateru, located in a garden in the inner precincts of Ise shrine (Kobayashi Issa 4.335, note 1). Since Issa wrote the poem in First Month in Shinano Province, 300 kilometers north of Ise shrine, he must have relied on memory or imagination when composing.[36] In any case, the poet's head, without conscious design or effort, drops in reverence to the hill and its indwelling deity, thus embodying Shinran's ideal of natural faith.

Issa is not the only person bowing to Nature inside his haiku. In a previously cited one, we see a great provincial lord humbling himself spontaneously to the spontaneous blossoms.

大名を馬からおろす桜哉
daimyō wo uma kara orosu sakura kana
(234.9)

a lord
forced off his horse . . .
cherry blossoms

We noted earlier that this haiku expresses a social irony. The normally groveled-to feudal lord now becomes, despite his status and power in the human world, the groveler. The cherry trees outrank him because, according to Shinto, they are sacred vessels of the gods. The daimyo's gesture is religious in nature, not histrionic, not forced. When he dismounts in deference to the blossoms, he is no more planning or controlling this action than is Issa when his head, "of itself," bows to Mount Kamiji.

Shinran's doctrine of non-calculating naturalness is evident throughout Issa's self-portraits.

のふなしはつみも又なし冬ごもり
nō nashi wa tsumi mo mata nashi fuyugomori
(699.20)

no good deeds
but also no sins . . .
winter seclusion

In his winter seclusion he has done nothing out of the ordinary, neither "good deeds" nor "sins." Blyth translates the first and middle phrases of the haiku, "Merit-less,/ And guilt-less" (*Haiku* 4.1249), suggesting that the poet has accumulated neither good nor bad karma.[37] As far as karmic merits and demerits go, Issa has been too lazy to earn either. On its surface, the haiku presents a moment of comic self-irony. Deeper, it evokes Shinran's recommendation that one not strive for the Pure Land. Issa's lackadaisical attitude represents a Jōdoshinshū ideal; being *kono mama*, "just as he is," he withdraws from the futile karmic struggle.

This withdrawal is the only sensible course of action (actually, inaction) in light of the inescapability of sin in the age of *mappō*.

米蒔くも罪ぞよ鶏がけあふぞよ

kome maku mo tsumi zoyo tori ga keau zoyo
(110.16)

even tossing rice
is a sin . . .
cockfight!

Compassion stirs Issa to feed the hungry birds, but doing so in the context of this fallen world of greed and craving twists his good deed into a "sin" (*tsumi*), for it causes a violent bout of kicking and pecking to break out among them. The haiku appears in *Shichiban nikki*, 1812, Second Month, with the prescript, "At Fuse [no] Benten" (3.150). That same year, Issa includes the haiku in another text with a more descriptive preamble.

On a temple-visit to Tōkaiji in Fuse [no Benten], chickens followed me inexpediently. At a house in front of the temple gate, I bought just a bit of rice [one *go*], which I scattered among the violets and dandelions. Before long though, a fight broke out. Meanwhile, groups of pigeons and sparrows came flying down from the branches, eating with tranquil hearts, but when the chickens returned, back to the trees they quickly fled. The pigeons and sparrows would have liked the kicking-fight to have lasted longer.

Samurai, farmers, artisans, and merchants all make their living in this manner. (6.52)

One *go* of rice is a mere .18 liter, yet the chickens go to war over it. The phrase that Issa uses, "samurai, farmers, artisans, and merchants" (*shinōkōshō*: 士農工商), is a Japanese expression that denotes feudal class distinctions. People from all four ranks scrape and struggle to fill their bellies . . . at the expense of others. Squabbling birds at a temple gate represent a microcosm of human society. In a fallen age driven by the tyranny of ego, every situation is fundamentally hopeless—even for those who try to do good.

We have seen how Issa at times uses butterflies as emblems of purity and detachment: air-light creatures that rise above the dust of worldliness. In one situation, however, even they seem caught up in petty jealousy and strife.

黄色組白組蝶の地どりけり
kiiro-gumi shiro-gumi chō no chidori keri
(172.16)

yellow gang, white gang
the butterflies stake
their claims

白黄色蝶も組合したりけり
shiro kiiro chō mo kumiai shitari keri (172.20)

white versus yellow—
the butterflies
wrestle too

In the first poem, yellow and white "gangs" claim their respective territories in a meadow. In the second, they grapple like wrestlers.[38] Their color-coded conflict pokes fun at sadly typical human behavior, like the birds squabbling for crumbs in the previous example. And, beyond this satirical point, Issa's battling butterflies embody the Pure Land Buddhist idea of sin's inescapability. If even the gentle butterflies covet and compete, what possible hope does anyone else have for attaining detachment and nirvana?

One haiku finds comedy in Shinran's dictum that sin is unavoidable.

山寺や祖師のゆるしの猫の恋

yamadera ya soshi no yurushi no neko no koi
(122.16)

mountain temple—
with the Founder's blessing
cats make love

The "Founder" is Shinran, who took a wife to dramatize the fact that all self-powered action, including the discipline of attempting to avoid lust through celibacy, has nothing to do with gaining enlightenment. Shinran married (he was the first Buddhist cleric in Japan to do so) because he believed that faith (*shinjin*: 信心) is more important than the outward practice of the *nembutsu*—a bold move for which he and his followers were attacked by older and more established Buddhist sects of the time, particularly by the militant Tendai priests of Mount Hiei (Dobbins 332-34). Despite this repression, Jōdoshinshū priests followed Shinran's example and have done so ever since, marrying if they choose. In Issa's comic reflection on this custom, felines are treated as fellow Buddhists who enjoy the same rights and privileges. The temple cats, too, enjoy Shinran's permission to copulate. Of course, they do not need it because, unlike their human counterparts, they guiltlessly follow their nature without calculation or qualm.

Shinran's embracing of meat-eating and clerical marriage (*nikujiki saitai:* 肉食妻帯) established the precedent for Issa's approach to sin. Whether one views the patriarch's policy as an admission of human weakness or, as the Buddhist scholar Chikū argues, "a willful act of compassion made by a manifestation of Amida," his followers, including Issa, live in a reality where sin is unavoidable and the only recourse is to stop striving against it (Jaffe 51). Accordingly, Issa's shabby and tumbledown house is less a reflection of laziness than it is of the natural, non-calculating philosophy which Shinran recommends in the age of *mappō*.

名月の御覧の通り屑家也

meigetsu no goran no tōri kuzuya nari
(455.25)

lit by the harvest moon
no different . . .
trashy house

Issa composed this haiku in 1808 while visiting some of his haiku students in Nojiri, a village located just to the north of Kashiwabara (2.481;

484). His inheritance had not yet been settled, so it is unlikely that the particular "trashy house" referred to in the haiku is his place of birth. Yet, years later, after settling in his half of the divided family homestead, he continues to describe his home as a "trashy house" (*kuzuya*)—a structure so fragile, he adds, the wind might blow it away at any moment (6.136). LaFleur points out that the hermit's hut symbolizes Buddhist transience in Japanese literary tradition: huts are impermanent abodes that embody the evanescent, fleeting quality of the universe (60). Beyond this, in the context of Pure Land Buddhism, Issa's unkempt, unswept, roof-leaking shack embodies Shinran's ideal of *jinen*, naturalness. There is no dressing it up, no putting on of airs, even on auspicious occasions.

あばら家や其身其まま明の春
abaraya ya sono mi sono mama kesa no haru
(27.14)

tumble-down house
no different
spring begins

元日も立のままなる屑哉
*ganjitsu mo tatsu no mama naru kuzuya
kana* (23.19)

New Year's Day—
no different
trashy house

元日も別条のなき屑屋哉

ganjitsu mo betsujō no naki kuzuya kana
(23.20)

a new year
but no change for
this trashy house

On the first day of the year and the beginning of spring, the poet's house is no different. In a prose passage in *Oraga haru*, he confesses that he has not bothered to decorate his hovel on New Year's Day with the traditional pine-and-bamboo decoration, nor has he swept its soot (6.136). This naturalness of Issa and his hut relates directly to the poet's Pure Land faith, particularly in its recommendation that calculated efforts cannot earn salvation. Trusting Amida Buddha and being "just as I am" are sufficient.

それなりに成仏とげよかたつぶり

sore nari ni jōbutsu toge yo katatsuburi
(386.8)

just as you are
become Buddha!
snail

それ也になる仏いたせ穴の蛇

sore nari ni narubutsu itase ana no hebi
(535.23)

just as you are
become Buddha!
snake in your hole

人ならば仏性なるなまこ哉
hito naraba hotoke shū naru namako kana
(722.22)

if they were people
they'd be Buddhas!
sea slugs

In Issa's view, snails, snakes, and even sea slugs are on the road to enlightenment precisely because they are not *trying* to be enlightened. Simply, naturally, they just are what they are.

The unthinking natural piety of animals is one of Issa's favorite themes, so examples are legion. For our purposes, two more will suffice.

さほしかの黙礼したり萩の花
saoshika no mokurei shitari hagi no hana
(573.8)

the young buck
silently bows . . .
blooming bush clover

念仏をさづけてやらん帰る雁
nembutsu wo sazukete yaran kaeru kari
(152.5)

teaching how to
praise Buddha . . .
the geese return

Most likely, the buck is bowing to the bush clover in order to devour it, but Issa's language suggests reverence and respect for Nature's gift of blossoms: so lovely, so delicious. The human Buddhist can learn much from the deer's unthinking bow. In similar fashion, the clamorous geese returning in springtime teach the inner truth of the *nembutsu*, not the human words *namu amida butsu* but rather the wildly uplifting, spontaneous spirit of the prayer: heartfelt and unpremeditated.

In light of the premium placed on being natural and non-forcing in Shinran's Buddhism, Issa chose his first wife well. Of Kiku he writes,

我菊や形にもふりにもかまはずに
waga kiku ya nari ni mo furi ni mo kama-
wazu ni (557.29)

my chrysanthemum
doesn't care about looks
or style.

The haiku can be read as a comment about a cultivated flower or, more personally, about Kiku ("Chrysanthemum") the woman. If we interpret it in the latter way, and we believe Issa's characterization of her, he and Kiku were a good match. Issa also cared little about looks or style in his "ramshackle house" (*abaraya*). Spiders lurking in its corners had nothing to fear from his broom.

隅の蜘案じな煤はとらぬぞよ
sumi no kumo anjina susu wa toranu zoyo
(669.13)

corner spider
rest easy, my soot-broom
is idle

Since he valued living his life *kono mama* ("just as I am"), Issa could have paid Kiku no higher compliment than to say that she, too, was unconcerned with outward appearances. Yet one can hardly help wondering if she tolerated spiders in the corners. This is one question on which the written record is silent.

The opening haiku of *Oraga haru*, from which the diary derives its name, is one of Issa's most well known expressions of naturalness.

目出度さもちう位也おらが春

medetasa mo chū kurai nari oraga haru
(29.16)

my "Happy New Year!"
about average . . .
my spring

He sets up the haiku with an anecdote.

At Fukō Temple in Tango Province, there once was a saintly priest who deeply longed for the Pure Land. As the celebration of the new year approached, on New Year's Eve, he gave a young priest a letter, instructing him, "Deliver this to me at the break of dawn tomorrow. Now, off you go to sleep in the temple hall."

On New Year's Day at dawn, while every nook and cranny was still a bit dark, and the first bird of the year was singing, the young priest came running. As instructed, he banged on the front gate. A voice from within asked, "Where are you from?"

"I bear a message from Amida Buddha of the West," came the reply, upon which the saintly priest, barefooted, rushed to the doors and threw them open, left and right. He led the young priest to the high seat of honor, and, taking yesterday's letter, reverently read, "Amid this world's abundance of distress, hurry and come to my land. My saints are waiting to greet you."

Finishing his reading, the saintly priest wept. (6.135)

Unlike the "saintly priest" of his story, Issa claims that he is "buried in worldly dust" (6.135), and yet there are similarities between them. Like the priest, he has an unconventional way of welcoming the new year. He will not place a pine-and-bamboo decoration on his gate, nor engage in any other special ceremonies of the season. He greets the new year just as he is, without fanfare, and so his New Year's greeting (*medetasa*) and his New Year's mood are "about average."

Issa and the priest are also alike in that they await Amida Buddha's grace "amid this world's abundance of distress." Since there is no way to earn that grace, according to Shinran, the best policy is to trust in Amida's Other Power and accept whatever life (and afterlife) brings.

長の日や沈香も焚かず屁もひらず
naga no hi ya jinkō mo takazu he mo hirazu
(62.20)

a long day—
not incense
not a fart

Literally, the haiku refers to the burning of fragrant aloes (*jinkō*). Issa perceives neither this pleasant odor nor that of a "fart" (*he*). His long day hasn't been good, hasn't been bad. Once again, he is not celebrating laziness or apathy, but, like a good Buddhist, accepting whatever is, including himself, *kono mama*.

   Although outsiders may have regarded his slovenly lifestyle and ramshackle hut with disapproval, Issa accepts both cheerfully.

時鳥俗な庵とさみするな
hototogisu zokuna iori to sami suruna
(341.10)

don't disdain
my worldly hut
cuckoo!

鶯の目利してなくわが家哉
uguisu no mekiki shite naku waga ya kana
(136.11)

with disdain
the nightingale critiques
my house

あばらやに痩がまんせぬぼたん哉

abaraya ni yasegaman senu botan kana
(395.17)

putting up
with the tumble-down house . . .
peony

Despite a cuckoo's disdain, a nightingale's criticism, or a peony's long suffering, the poet makes no attempts to tidy up the place. He lets his hut stay as it is, and he even accepts its leaking roof with Buddhist composure.

御盛りや草の庵ももりはじめ

osagari ya kusa no iori mo mori hajime
(33.25)

the year's first rain—
my grass roof's
first leak

The holes in the walls and windows turn out to be unexpected amenities, for they allow glimpses of sky and can even create music.

壁の穴や我初空もうつくしき

kabe no ana ya waga hatsuzora mo utsuku-shiki (32.22)

hole in the wall
pretty
my year's first sky

秋の夜や窓の小穴が笛を吹

aki no yo ya mado no ko ana ga fue wo fuku

(445.1)

autumn evening—
a little hole in the window
blows flute

We have already noted that Shinran's valuing of *kono mama* ("being just as I am") derives in part from the Taoism of ancient China (Bloom, *Shinran's Gospel* 43-44). A corollary to naturalness is the concept of balance—the Yin and the Yang. Issa devotes the same open-minded, accepting, non-calculating, and non-forcing attention to great and small, pretty and ugly, rich and poor, perfume and fart. In his poetic vision, a mountain is no more significant or worthy of note than a fly is.

蠅一つ打ては山を見たりけり

hae hitotsu utte wa yama wo mitari keri

(373.4)

swatting a fly
looking at
a mountain

A lovely flower shares the spotlight with a pile of dung.

菊さくや馬糞山も一けしき

kiku saku ya ma-guso yama mo hito keshiki

(556.33)

chrysanthemum blooming
horse-shit mountain . . .
one scene

In the haiku that immediately follows the above
one in *Shichiban nikki*, Issa brings the flower and
the horse manure together even more dramat-
ically.

夕暮や馬糞の手をも菊でふく
yūgure ya ma-guso no te wo mo kiku de fuku
(557.5)

evening—
wiping horse shit off the hands
with a mum

Anyone who peruses Issa's works soon discovers
that his poetic vision embraces more than
pleasant scenes of flowers and moon. His blunt
realism, his attending to the world's excrement as
much as to its butterflies, flows naturally from a
Buddhist acceptance of what is: the Yin and the
Yang.

雀らよ小便無用古衾
suzume-ra yo shōben muyō furu fusuma
(691.17)

hey sparrows—
no pissing on my old
winter quilt!

Shōben is a euphemism in Japanese, a combi-
nation of the words "little" and "convenience." I

have translated it as "pissing" in an attempt to capture the humor of the poem.[39] In a variant form of this haiku, Issa substitutes *nezumi-ra*, mice, for the sparrows.

鼠らよ小便無用古衾
nezumi-ra yo shōben muyō furu fusuma
(691.17, variant)

hey mice—
no pissing on my old
winter quilt!

Another haiku refers to cicada piddle.

初蝉といへば小便したりけり
hatsu semi to ieba shōben shitari keri
(382.24)

"first cicada!"
he says
while it pisses

Someone notices a cicada when, in almost the same instant, something else happens: the insect makes water. The French translator, Collet, pictures the speaker to be Issa and so renders the first part of the middle phrase, *to ieba*, as *dis-je*: "I say" (99). Blyth has a third person ("he") make the announcement (*History* 1.367). An even thornier translation problem is identifying the piddler in the haiku. Blyth and Collet decide that a human speaker is doing his business; Blyth remarks that this noticing of Nature while following one's own captures "the meaningfulness of accident" (367). My Japanese informant Shinji Ōgawa, however, pictures a different sort of accident. He notes, "It is a well known fact by those boys who chase cicadas on a hot summer day that cicadas piss quite often." He imagines that the speaker of the poem is an excited boy who looks up to see a cicada flying from one tree trunk to another only to get showered in the face: a comic image that shows the weird balance of Yin and Yang in Issa. Refined poetic feeling—the heralding of summer's first cicada—coexists in the same poem with potty humor.

The sublime and the mundane live side by side in the haiku of Issa.

船頭よ小便無用浪の月
sendō yo shōben muyō nami no tsuki
(449.18)

hey boatman
no pissing on the moon
in the waves!

小便の香も通ひけり菊の花
shōben no ka mo kayoi keri kiku no hana
(557.21)

the smell of piss
wafting too . . .
chrysanthemums

小便のたらたら下や杜若
shōben no tara-tara dare ya kakitsubata
(402.17)

where piss dribbles,
dribbles down . . .
irises

小便の穴だらけ也残り雪
shōben no ana darake nari nokori yuki (98.6)

riddled with piddle
the last
snow pile

The natural purity of moon, chrysanthemums,
irises, and snow commingle with the just-as-
natural piddle. On one level, these haiku perform
as jokes, ironic juxtapositions that shock the
reader with the unexpected. Beneath their surface, however, Issa hints of the corrupt, present
age of *mappō* in which beauty and purity cannot
abide. However, despite this troubling undertone,
the general mood in these haiku is one of quiet,
smiling acceptance. At times he smiles sadly,
other times happily, but always, it seems, Issa
smiles.

The Japanese critic, Fujimoto, observes, "Issa,
without concern, makes poems about unsightly,
unclean, shameful things . . . such topics seem
neither chopsticks nor canes [i.e., they are good
for nothing], yet Issa encounters them with
interest" (500). Fujimoto quotes the above-cited
piddle-riddled snow pile haiku as an example of a
"dirty" (*kitanai*) poem. Another example that he
cites is the following.

大川へ虱とばする美人哉
ōkawa e shirami tobasuru bijin kana (381.1)

into the big river
tossing her lice . . .
pretty woman

The woman is beautiful but has lice; she is attractive but cruel. Yin and Yang, good and bad, yes and no—arise together . . . naturally. Issa portrays the balance of such oppositions with nonjudgmental realism.

According to Kaneko Tohta, Issa captures moments of everyday life that earlier haiku masters, such as Bashō and Buson, did not regard as proper for poetry. Kaneko cites the following haiku as an example of the type of poem that Bashō and Buson would not write (228-29).

夕顔の花で洟かむ娘かな

yūgao no hana de hana kamu musume kana
(391.8)

blowing her snot
on the moonflower . . .
a young girl

Issa plays with the homonyms *hana* ("flower" 花) and *hana* ("snot" 洟). The image of a girl using a delicate, white flower as her snot-rag is hardly refined, but it is realistic. Issa revises this haiku in *Oraga haru*.

夕顔の花で洟かむおば[ば]哉

yūgao no hana de hana kamu o-ba[ba] kana
(391.8, variant)

blowing her snot
on the moonflower . . .
grandma

Now an old woman (*o-baba*) defiles the blossom.
The comedy of the two versions differs in subtle
ways. In the first, the girl seems innocently
egocentric; in the later haiku, "grandma" seems
crass and indifferent. Either way, the scene is
funny, real, and natural.[40]

Issa's poetry and lifestyle in his "trashy
house" involve a profound acceptance of the
unadorned, the uncensored, the natural, and the
spontaneous. Majestic mountain and pesky fly,
chrysanthemums and horse dung, snow and piddle, moonflower and snot; such odd yet realistic
juxtapositions express the poet's acceptance of
the universe and of himself within that universe:
kono mama . . . just as they are.

Issa also depicts naturalness in this well-
known haiku based on a Buddhist legend.

春風や牛に引かれて善光寺
harukaze ya ushi ni hikarete zenkōji (76.9)

spring breeze—
a cow leads the way
to Zenkō Temple

The haiku appears first in *Shichiban nikki*, a
Second Month entry of 1811 (3.108). Issa
recopied it in *Waga haru shū* ("My Spring
Collection") with the prescript, "From the 25th
day of Second Month, Buddha's image exhibited"
(6.24). The exhibition of Amida Buddha's image at

Zenkōji, the major temple in Issa's home province of Shinano, attracts throngs of visiting pilgrims. In the case of this haiku, the traveler, following a cow, becomes a pilgrim too, but unaware of this fact. Blyth recounts Issa's source story.

> In a certain village, not far from Zenkōji, there lived an old woman who had no belief in religion, had never been to Zenkōji and could not be persuaded to go there. One day, a piece of white cloth which she had hung out to dry on the fence of the back garden, caught on the horn of a passing ox, and when she ran after it the animal made off. However far she followed it, she could not catch it, and at length they got to Zenkōji. The ox seemed to disappear, and when she looked around in surprise, she saw that she was standing before the image of Nyorai. At this, she felt for the first time that spirit of veneration which is the beginning and foundation of all faith, and became a firm believer. (*Haiku* 2.422-23)

The way to Amida's Pure Land does not depend on ego-driven calculation. In a later version, Issa substitutes a butterfly for the cow.

此方が善光寺とや蝶のとぶ

kono kata ga zenkōji to ya chō no tobu

(170.7)

"Follow me to Zenkō Temple!"
a butterfly
flies

The road to enlightenment takes many forms in Issa's haiku, but always the common denominator is naturalness. One might arrive there by following a butterfly or a runaway cow, or perhaps, simply, by opening one's eyes and taking in whatever the universe provides—beautiful women, lice, flowers, snot, snow, piddle—with non-grasping, non-judging, deep and abiding acceptance. Slovenly Issa and his slovenly hut appear just as they are: not striving, not planning, not putting on airs . . . not calculating. His head without forethought bows "of itself" to the world's peonies and sacred hills, while his heart-mind (*kokoro:* 心) remains an empty cup that Amida Buddha rushes to fill, for only in such hearts and minds does saving grace come pouring in.

Chapter 6. *EN:* Karma

Shortly before he died, Shinran wrote the following note to a friend: "Even when my life comes to an end and I am reborn into the Pure Land, I will come back again and again, like the waves dashing on the beach of Waka-no-ura" (Tran. Kurata 246). Reincarnation, especially in relation to the bodhisattva myth of enlightened beings returning to the world of suffering to enlighten others, was a favorite theme for the founder of Jōdoshinshū and, consequently, for his followers. Issa writes, then rewrites, a haiku about himself and a butterfly under a shady tree.

木の陰や蝶と休むも他生の縁

ki no kage ya chō to yasumu mo tashō no en

(175.11)

in tree shade
relaxing with a butterfly . . .
friends in a previous life

木の陰やてふと宿るも他生の縁

ki no kage ya chō to yadoru mo tashō no en

(175.11, variant)

sharing tree shade
with a butterfly . . .
friends in a previous life

The word *tashō* (他生) in the third phrase of both versions denotes a previous life, while *en* (縁) signifies karma. The Buddhist concept of *tashō no en* ("previous life's karma") provides the poet with a mythic explanation for the connection he feels: How else to explain his sense of recognition and relationship? He and the butterfly *must* have been on good terms in a previous lifetime.[41] With their slightly different middle-phrase verbs—*yasumu* (rest, relax) versus *yadoru* (lodge, stop, dwell)—the poems evoke a sweet, delicate moment, and that should be enough for the appreciative reader. However, as often is the case with Issa, there's more to the story, for this butterfly isn't *only* a butterfly. The first version appears in *Bunsei kuchō* ("Bunsei Era Haiku Notebook") in a Second Month, 1825 entry; the undated revision is found in *Issa hokku shū* ("Issa's Haiku Collection"). In both texts Issa includes prose prescripts. In *Issa hokku shū*, he writes, "A little girl was serving as my guide on a mountain road, when a capricious rain suddenly fell" (4.530), and in *Bunsei kuchō*, he reveals still more: "Being guided on a mountain road by a young girl named Butterfly, a sudden rain came pattering down" (1.175). The "butterfly" in the scene, then, is an insect if the poem is read in isolation but a little girl when it is read alongside the prose introductions. As Issa crouches under a tree in the rain with this insect/girl, he senses their karmic connection from an earlier life.[42]

When the writers of *The Princeton Companion to Classical Japanese Literature* refer condescendingly to Issa's "sentimentality" (Miner 94), they might be well advised to take a close look at these butterfly poems and others like it.[43] Issa's tender feelings toward insects, children, birds, and flowers arise within a context of his Buddhist understanding of life and the essential connectedness of sentient beings. When he treats animals as peers, critics label this "personification" and label him a "child's poet." Yet Issa's portrayal of non-human beings as conscious, aware colleagues seems not quite childish or sentimental when one sees this in terms of his belief in reincarnation and karma, core values of his Jōdoshinshū faith. In the above examples and the one that follows, his sense of kinship with fellow creatures is not a silly affectation but rather a genuine emotion of the type that any family member might feel for another.

前の世のおれがいとこか閑古鳥

saki no yo no orega itoko ka kankodori
(348.18)

in a previous
life, my cousin?
mountain cuckoo

The mountain cuckoo (*kankodori*) epitomizes the laid-back, relaxing, do-nothing days of summer, and as such is the perfect foil for "lazy-bones" Issa. In addition, the same bird warbling among the cedars is, like Issa, a poet.

俳諧を囀るやうなかんこ鳥

haikai wo saezuru yōna kankodori (349.7)

like warbling pure haiku
mountain
cuckoo

They are such kindred spirits they *must* have been related in an earlier life. Were they, perhaps, first cousins (*itoko*) Issa wonders? If so, they remain cousins and retain something of their family resemblance—though one of them now has feathers—in the present life. These haiku with their portraits of a "cousin" cuckoo gushing one-breath poems are comic in tone, and yet their undertone is patently serious. Issa and the cuckoo *are* cousins in a Buddhist worldview. Moreover, the fact that the poet is human in no way privileges him or sets him above his animal kin. Issa does not subscribe to a notion of linear improvement in reincarnation: that one progresses from "lower" forms such as trees and flowers to "higher" animal forms, then on to human form and, ultimately, to awakening as a Buddha. He postulates no such bottom-to-top karmic ladder. Indeed, his being reborn as a butterfly, he suggests in one haiku, would be just fine.

むつまじや生れかはらばのべの蝶

mutsumaji ya umare kawaraba nobe no chō
(168.2)

such sweet harmony
to be reborn
a meadow butterfly![44]

The concept of *mappō* provides an unspoken framework for Issa's reverie. The meadow butterflies are "harmonious" and "friendly" (*mutsumaji*), and so being reborn as one would represent a definite karmic improvement over human existence in this ego-ruined, corrupt age. A haiku cited earlier bears repeating in this regard.

蝶とぶや此世に望みないやうに

chō tobu ya kono yo ni nozomi nai yō ni
(167.17)

a butterfly flits
as if wanting nothing
in this world

Because they lack the human heart with its tendency to covet and the human brain with its drive to calculate in the service of covetousness, Issa's animal cousins are somewhat better off than humans, karmically speaking, and so serve as role models in his poetry, embodying a better way of being in the world: guileless, non-striving, and living in the moment.

稲妻や狗ばかり無欲顔

inazuma ya enokoro bakari muyoku kao
(485.16)

lightning flash—
only the puppy's face
is innocent

According to Buddhist tradition, there are "Six Ways" (*rokudō:* 六道) of future life reincarnation:

as a sufferer in hell, as a hungry ghost, as an animal, as an angry demon, as a human being, and as a heavenly being. While the sixth of these Six Realms remains the universal goal, Issa maintains that the third realm, animal existence, is a lucky one. This belief is evident in a six-haiku series that he writes on the Six Ways in the 1812 book, *Kabuban*, in which the following haiku appears with the prescript "Beasts" (*chikushō:* 畜生; 6.48).

ちる花に仏とも法ともしらぬ哉
chiru hana ni butsu tomo nori tomo shiranu kana (212.10)

in scattering blooms
Buddha and Buddhism
unknown

Animals are ignorant of Buddha and Buddha's dharma-law (*nori*), and yet, ironically, Issa does not portray this as a problem. Immersed in a transient universe where flowers and all living things scatter to oblivion, they do not realize this fact but instead live in the moment without calculating . . . or clinging. Their here-and-now, no-fretting existence recalls Walt Whitman's admiring portrayal in *Leaves of Grass*.

I think I could turn and live with animals,
they're so placid and self-contain'd,
I stand and look at them long and long.
They do not sweat and whine about their
condition,

They do not lie awake in the dark and weep
for their sins,
They do not make me sick discussing their
duty to God . . . (47)

Like his American counterpart, Issa holds the
utmost respect for animals, "so placid and self-
contain'd." But for Issa this respect is grounded
in Buddhism with its doctrines of karma and
mappō, constructs that provide the semantic
context for his anthropomorphic treatment of
animals. Critics who detect soft-hearted sentimentality in a haiku like the following are missing
the boat.

やれ打な蝿が手をすり足をする
yare utsuna hae ga te wo suri ashi wo suru
(375.16)

don't swat the fly!
wringing hands
wringing feet

Kaneko Tohta classifies the poem as *jihi no ku* (慈
悲の句)—a haiku of mercy, benevolence, and compassion (264). However, it is important to re-
member the karmic understanding from which
such tenderness arises.

慈悲すれば糞をする也雀の子
jihi sureba hako wo suru nari suzume no ko
(130.24)

when you hold him kindly
he poops on you . . .
baby sparrow

春雨や喰れ残りの鴨が鳴

harusame ya kuware-nokori no kamo ga
naku (70.14)

spring rain—
the uneaten ducks
are quacking

こおろぎの寒宿とする衾哉

kōrogi no kanshuku to suru fusuma kana
(691.1)

the cricket's
winter residence
my quilt

Issa treats the baby sparrow with tender mercy (*jihi*) and is rewarded with poop in his hand. Yet he expresses neither disgust not regret; his hand remains open and accepting of his little fellow traveler and its gifts. Similarly, he empathizes with those ducks that have survived the cooking pots of winter; he celebrates their celebration. Their joy of being alive in the pouring spring rain becomes Issa's joy—and the reader's. In the third example, a winter poem, a cricket moves into its "cold weather home" (*kanshuku*): Issa's bedding. But instead of treating it like a nuisance, the poet welcomes the tiny new arrival as an honored guest.

Given the fact that Issa regards animals as karmic cousins on the road to enlightenment, his habit of addressing them directly in haiku seems only natural.

狭くともいざ飛習へ庵の蚤

semaku to mo iza tobinarae io no nomi
(378.2)

though it's cramped
practice your jumping
hut's fleas

留主にするぞ恋して遊べ庵の蝿

rusu ni suru zo koi shite asobe io no hae
(374.3)

while I'm away
enjoy your lovemaking
hut's flies

寝返りをするぞそこのけきりぎりす

negaeri wo suru zo soko noke kirigirisu
(549.14)

turning over in bed—
move aside!
katydid

白露の玉ふみかくなきりぎりす

shira tsuyu no tama fumikaku na kirigirisu
(549.10)

don't crush
the dewdrop pearls!
katydid[45]

About the last example, Blyth writes, "This is the natural attitude of the tender-minded poet . . . [who], as such, disturbs nothing, not even the dew-drops on the morning grass" (*Haiku* 4.1068-69). I prefer to view this haiku and the hundreds of others like it differently. Issa is not so much "tender-minded" as he is a practitioner of Buddhism for whom animals are colleagues to be loved, chided, or, when he rolls over in bed, given fair warning. In another haiku involving a katydid (a cousin to grasshoppers and crickets), he warns of an impending shower.

小便をするぞ退け退けきりぎりす
shōben wo suru zo noke noke kirigirisu
(550.2)

I'm taking a leak
so look out!
katydid

Using similar diction, he offers a baby sparrow some friendly advice.

雀の子そこのけそこのけ御馬が通る
suzume no ko soko noke soko noke o-uma ga tōru (130.9)

baby sparrows
move aside!
Sir Horse passes

Though Japanese school children are made to memorize it, this haiku is no mere child's poem. It not only vocalizes Issa's Buddhist compassion for, and sense of karmic connection with, sentient life; it hints of a political meaning. The "honorable horse" (*o-uma*) comes stomping by without thought for the baby sparrow in its path, and so the poem might be viewed as a gentle satire on how feudal lords relate to "mere" peasants. The first lesson of the haiku for sparrows and humans alike is one in the same: step out of the way of worldly power . . . or be crushed. The second lesson, a religious one, is implicit in the poet's direct way of speaking to the little bird (or birds): an artificial distinction between "lower" and "higher" forms of life does not apply to cousins.

In another example, Issa makes an inquiry of a snail as if he fully expects an answer.

朝やけがよろこばしいかかたつぶり

asayake ga yorokobashii ka katatsuburi
(385.17)

does the red dawn
delight you
snail?

Of course, the poem expresses Issa's own feeling of delight at the dawn colors. Cannot a snail also enjoy such this spectacle, he wonders? In a later revision he substitutes "red sunset" (*yūyake*) for "red dawn" in the opening phrase (1.385), but whether the sun is rising or setting, he and the snail are perfectly equal colleagues in the haiku moment.

Issa addresses a Japanese nigthingale or *uguisu* with the words of a famous medieval samurai.

時鳥蝿虫めらもよっく聞け

hototogisu hae mushimera mo yokku kike
(344.19)

cuckoo
"O flies and worms
listen well!"

In *Oraga haru*, the prescript reads, "In the place where Chinzei Hachirō Tametomo tossed people like small stones" (6.152). Chinzei Hachirō Tametomo was a twelfth century warrior, a peerless archer and formidable strongman (6.173, note 239). Yuasa describes him as "a seven-foot Hercules" (113). In the haiku, Issa parodies his battle cry: "From cuckoos down to demons, listen well!" In a delightful twist, these heroic words serve fair warning to all flies and *mushi* (worms and other crawling bugs) that Sir Cuckoo is here, so beware! Casting the *hototogisu* as a powerful samurai vis-à-vis insects and worms makes for a delightful moment of haiku comedy. The old battlefield proves to be a battlefield still, the war cry of a cuckoo alerting all *mushi* within earshot before the morning's carnage begins. Six years later, Issa reworks the image in a haiku that we have looked at earlier in this book.

無常鐘蝿虫めらもよっくきけ

mujō-gane hae mushimera mo yokku kike
(376.20)

the bell of life passing—
O flies and worms
listen well!

This time it is a temple bell signaling life's transience (*mujō*) to which the buzzing and creeping
things are told to pay heed.

Issa addresses another animal, this time a
cuckoo, with similarly stilted and literary language.

我汝を待こと久し時鳥

ware nanji wo matsu koto hisashi hototogisu
(338.18)

I've waited long
for thee
O cuckoo!

This haiku was composed in Fourth Month, 1810.
Later, Issa recopies it several times with explan-
atory prescripts. In Third Month 1817 and in
Oraga haru (1819), he writes, "A painting of an
old man sitting on a rock handing over a scroll"
(3.472; 6.152). In Fourth Month 1817, one word
is changed but the basic meaning remains the
same: "The place where an old man sitting on a
rock handed over a scroll" (3.475). According to

tradition, Kōsekikō met Chōryō at Kahi Bridge, where the former conferred upon the latter a scroll containing his tactics of war. Chōryō arrived late, and was greeted by the old man with the words, "I've waited long for thee!" Issa humorously applies this famous historical quote to his present situation. He has waited long to hear the song of the tardy cuckoo, whom he chides.

A haiku addressing a toad also has historical resonance.

> 蟇どのの妻や待らん子鳴らん
> *hiki dono no tsuma ya matsuran ko nakuran*
> (355.12)

> Mister Toad—
> the wife may be waiting
> your children crying

In this verse, Issa parodies a *waka* written by Yamanoue Okura, a Japanese poet who lived in the late seventh, early eighth centuries. On the occasion of leaving a banquet, Yamanoue composed a poem containing the lines, "My child must be crying/ and its mother . . . must be waiting for me" (Tran. Levy 186). Issa imitates this *waka* of the medieval *Man'yōshū* anthology with comic effect, applying the language of one of Japan's old, grand poets to a toad.

Issa does not always employ high brow literary allusions in his dealings with animals. In one case, he adopts the language of the playground.

雀子や女の中の豆いりに

suzumego ya onna no naka no mame iri ni
(130.13)

"Baby sparrow's
a sissy!"
playing with the girls

A literal translation of the haiku, "Baby sparrow—
among the women, a bean parching" makes no
sense in English. As Fujimoto points out, the
poem expresses a children's idiom (438), which
the editors of *Issa zenshū* explicate: "When a boy
is playing with girls, the expression, 'Among the
women, a bean parching,' is a form of teasing
banter" (4.136, note 1). Issa teases the sparrow as
if both of them are little boys, making the scene of
a 58 year-old man stooping to address a sparrow
even more incongruous and funny. Yet, as always
is the case with his animal interactions, the
subtext of the poem is that he and the baby sparrow are peers.

    At times, Issa's animals turn tables and
address him.

小便所ここと馬呼[ぶ]夜寒哉

shōbenjo koko to uma yo[bu] yosamu kana
(437.20)

"Here's the outhouse!"
the horse calls . . .
a cold night

Composed in *Hachiban nikki*, this haiku reappears in *Oraga haru* with the prescript, "Being lost at the time" (6.155). The editors of *Issa zenshū* speculate that Issa was staying at an unfamiliar house; walking outside to relieve himself in the darkness, he went astray (6.174). The kind horse, neighing in the night, helped him to get his bearings.

In Issa's universe, horses, birds, toads, flies, worms, snails, katydids, fleas, crickets, ducks, dogs, butterflies . . . all are cousins and companions on the karmic road to the Pure Land. As such, it is only natural that they, like Issa, should chant the *nembutsu* prayer in praise of Amida Buddha and his vow to rescue sentient beings.

> なむなむと蛙も石に並びけり
> *namu-namu to kawazu mo ishi ni narabi keri*
> (163.17)
>
> they praise Buddha too—
> frogs on a rock
> in a row
>
> なむなむと田にも並んでなく蛙
> *namu-namu to ta ni mo narande naku*
> *kawazu* (163.18)
>
> praising Buddha
> in a row in a rice field . . .
> frogs

We noted in the previous chapter, in a haiku

about geese (152.5), that animals embody Shinran's ideal of unthinking spontaneity enough to teach the *nembutsu* to their human counterparts. Here, the raucous cries of frogs in springtime do not merely parody a holy chant: for Issa, their prayer is genuine.

His animal comrades are not only good Buddhists, they piously revere the gods of Japan.

陽炎の猫にもたかる歩行神

kagerō no neko ni mo takaru aruki-gami
(92.6)

cats in the heat-shimmers
also follow
the God of Wandering[46]

寒月や雁も金毘羅祈る声

kan tsuki ya kari mo kompira inoru koe
(620.19)

cold moon—
wild geese, too, pray
to Kompira[47]

In the first poem, the word "also" (*mo*) indicates that someone else, unspecified in the poem, is involved; that person is, most likely, that inveterate "Cloud-Water" traveler, Issa. He, too, has been drawn to the road by the *aruki-gami*, God of Wandering, a deity that the editors of *Issa zenshū* describe as one who "entices people involuntarily to walk about" (3.350, note 2). Issa and the cats are filled with the same wanderlust, stirred by and devoted to the same divine force to roam . . . while heat shimmers bend and warp the air. The second example invokes Kompira, a powerful Shinto mountain god and protector of sailors and travelers. Issa imagines that the geese are raising their clamor in prayer for a safe journey. Once again, the particle *mo* ("too") implies that someone else is traveling and praying, and, once again, this unidentified someone is, presumably, Issa.

Animals are not the only beings that Issa acknowledges as peers and fellow travelers. Plant life is just as respected and as humanly treated. Cherry blossoms, for example, have awareness and feeling in his poetry, reacting emotionally when their admirers come calling.

人声にぼっとしたやら夕桜
hitogoe ni botto shita yara yūzakura (229.13)

at the sound of voices
evening cherry blossoms
blush

An alternative translation of this haiku is the following.

at the sound of voices
evening cherry blossoms
sigh

Two versions of the middle-seven phrase appear in *Issa zenshū*: *botto shita yara* ("blushed"; 3.296) and *hotto shita yara* ("sighed" or "felt disgust"; 1.229). Some translators depict the blossoms as if they are coquettish ladies, flushing a deeper shade of pink when they hear people's voices. Others, like Maruyama Kazuhiko, believe that the cherry blossoms are sighing with disgust, perhaps annoyed by the crowds invading their tranquil grove (206, note 1070). Either way, Issa's flowers emote. They, as much as humans, possess consciousness and are, therefore, future Buddhas, for, as Issa comments in *Oraga haru*, "even the trees and plants . . . will acquire Buddha-nature" (6.137). It is not surprising, then, to find him interacting with plants as sympathetically as he does with animals. An old pine is on the path to enlightenment.

仏ともならでうかうか老の松
hotoke tomo narade uka-uka oi no matsu
(744.1)

not yet Buddha—
the mindless old
pine

Blyth translates *uka-uka* as "idly dreaming" (*Haiku* 3.845). The pine tree manifests the detachment and non-mindedness that indicate it is well on the way to becoming a Buddha. An alternative reading of the haiku accepts *uka-uka* in its secondary meaning, denoting restlessness (Nakada 182). Agitated by the wind, the pine fails to show the perfect serenity of the Buddha it will one day become. Either way, the tree is a kindred spirit on the road to salvation, as are the wild roses in this haiku.

下々国の茨も正覚とりにけり

gege koku no bara mo shōgaku tori ni keri
(425.1)

even wild roses
of a downtrodden land
reach enlightenment

The "downtrodden land" (*gege koku*) is Issa's
impoverished home province of Shinano. The wild
roses might generally represent the thorny common folk of the land, or, more particularly, Issa
himself. Even a "wild rose" like he can one day
attain Buddha status. However, in addition to
this metaphorical reading, the wild roses in the
haiku literally *will* attain enlightenment.

Not only can plants realize enlightenment in
Issa's poetry, some of them serve to enlighten
others.

上人は菩薩と見たる桜哉
shōnin wa bosatsu to mitaru sakura kana
(227.3)

to saintly eyes
they are bodhisattvas . . .
cherry blossoms

A bodhisattva (*bosatsu*) is a Buddhist saint who
has returned to the world on a compassionate
mission to awaken others. When such a holy man
gazes upon the delicate, lovely cherry blossoms,
he perceives them as fellow saints with the power

to lead others to enlightenment. For Issa, plants are role models for Jōdoshinshū non-striving. "Just being alive" is good enough for a poppy and a poet.

生て居るばかりぞ我とけし[の]花
ikite iru bakari zo ware to heshi [no] hana
(392.16)

just being alive—
I
and the poppy

And the sublime indifference of a nettle tree is worth a thousand sermons on the Buddhist themes of detachment and "of itself" naturalness.

けろけろと師走月よの榎哉
kero-kero to shiwasu tsuki yo no enoki kana
(605.12)

indifferent
under a Twelfth Month moon . . .
nettle tree[48]

In Issa's opinion, creatures who have no concept of "Buddha" or "dharma" or "enlightenment" find themselves closer to all three than the most senior scholar-monks.

けさ秋としらぬ狗が仏哉
kesa aki to shiranu enoko ga hotoke kana
(430.31)

not knowing that
autumn's begun, puppy
Buddha!

立秋もしらぬ童が仏哉
tatsu aki mo shiranu warabe ga hotoke kana
(430.3)

not knowing that
autumn's begun, a child
Buddha!

The puppy and the child are karmically advanced not despite their ignorance of autumn's beginning—a symbol of *mujō*—but because of it. They revel innocently in the present moment without anxiety about autumn, loss, or the inevitable end of things. They are not Buddhists but Buddhas, and as such, Issa suggests, their way of being in the world is worth emulating.

In a playful mood, he writes about a flea that is also *en route* to nirvana.

あばれ蚤我手にかかって成仏せよ
abare nomi waga te kakate jōbutsu seyo
(377.8)

pesky flea
caught in my hand
become a Buddha!

This comic haiku offers a tongue-in-cheek defense for a flagrant violation of Buddha's precept against taking life: the rather lame excuse that he has done so only for his victim's benefit. On a deeper level, however, it is not inconsistent with Issa's view of the universe and karma to perceive that the guileless flea is truly Pure Land-bound. In another haiku, a flea's random hop lands it in a lucky place.

蚤とぶや笑仏の御口へ
nomi tobu ya warai-botoke no ōkuchi e
(377.5)

a flea jumps
in the laughing Buddha's
mouth

Because it isn't aiming for the Buddha, it hits the mark and so embodies Shinran's value of *jinen*: a natural, non-calculating "leap" of faith.

Karma is a major theme running throughout Issa's journals and poems. At times it surfaces in haiku as a mentioned topic; more often it lurks just beneath the surface of texts as subtext, situating references to animals and plants in a Buddhist semantic universe. Such references, viewed out of context, seem to confirm the stereotype of Issa as a sappy-sentimental "childs' poet." However, like his English contemporary, William Blake, whose *Songs of Innocence and Experience* were originally considered to be mere nursery rhymes before scholars began plumbing their deep waters; Issa has been dismissed too soon by too many. Like Blake, he has a genius for expressing profound and subtle insights in simple language. His poetic encounters with insects, birds, plants, and even "Sir Horse," when examined in relation to Buddhism and the doctrine of karma, broaden in significance not only to delight but to challenge his most adult, most sophisticated readers.

Chapter 7. *NEMBUTSU, TARIKI:* Prayer and Grace

The founder of Jōdoshinshū Buddhism, Shinran, identifies two major impediments to achieving enlightenment in the present, corrupt age of *mappō:* attachment and doubt. He explains,

> Nothing is like attachment in obstructing one's view; nothing is like doubt in concealing one's [light]. Let these two minds, attachment and doubt, be thoroughly cleared away. Then we shall find that there has never been anything keeping us away from the gate of the Pure Land. Amida's great Original Prayer will ever be by itself holding us up and taking care of us. (*Kyōgyōshinshō*, Tran. Suzuki 123)

The Pure Land is accessible even amid the depravity of this age and world only if one can make a leap of faith, trusting in Amida Buddha's "Original Prayer." Paradise, then, is not so much a physical place located in the distant west as it is a metaphor for awakening: the realization of enlightenment here and now. When one trusts in the "Other Power" of Amida, Shinran writes, that power sweeps one instantly to the Pure Land, after which the awakened person returns to the land of defilement (9). The Pure Land is not a resting place but a point of new beginning from which the enlightened individual, now in the role of bodhisattva, returns to the world of suffering on a mission to awaken others. Compassion demands this return, but it is not a return to delusion, attachment, or doubt. Shinran's enlightenment is non-retrogressive. Enlightened people are in this world but not *of* it; like the lotus blossom, they float on muddy water unmuddied.

That Issa was intimately familiar with the subtleties of Shinran's doctrine is nowhere more evident than in a prose passage found at the end of his 1819 poetic journal, *Oraga haru*, in which he puts forth his ideas on Buddhist salvation. He begins with a discussion of "other-powered" (*tariki*) versus "self-powered" (*jiriki*) salvation (6.156): "People who adhere to other-powered salvation but who do not truly trust in the strength of the Other Power, end up binding themselves with ropes of Other-Powered faith, falling into the blaze of their self-powered hell" (6.156). Belief in saving grace has its psychological pitfalls. Issa decries those Pure Land Buddhists who effectively only pay lip-service to Amida's power and in the process unwittingly bind themselves all the more tightly to the ego and its calculations. They have not truly trusted in Amida Buddha, for which their reward is "the blaze of . . . self-powered hell."

Issa goes on to describe a second doomed approach to salvation: "And then there are the soiled, ordinary men of clay, not blessed with Buddha's beautiful, golden body, growing old while they await the salvation order of Amida Buddha, but no such order is given . . . Even if they revoke evil, these are the very ring leaders of self-power" (6.156). Issa's word choice here is interesting. Ordinary men and women of clay (*dobombu:* 土凡夫) who do nothing but patiently await Amida's command to bring about their salvation, also lack genuine faith in the Buddha's Other Power. Such smug, do-nothing Buddhists are, he claims, the "ring leaders (*chōhonnin:* 張本人)" of self-power.

It is bad to rely on Amida Buddha without sincerity; it is bad to *expect* salvation. Yet this dilemma can be solved "without difficulty," Issa claims: "Though completely adrift on the open sea, one should regard the one great thing of the next life with unconcern; whether one is cast before the Buddha—to Hell or to Paradise—it is best to leave all to 'Thy will,' and simply trust" (6.156). The answer, then, is to go beyond doubt and passivity and submit to Amida Buddha with an attitude of "Thy will be done." By surrendering to this "Other Power"—not a deity but rather the embodiment of one's deepest, authentic reality; the Buddha beyond the fictive ego—one lets this power, as only it can, determine one's karmic fate.

This submission to the beyond, which Issa describes with the phrase "simply trust" (*o-tanomi mōsu bakari:* 御頼み申すばかり), is a transforming experience. He writes,

> Rather than the mouth reciting *namu amida butsu* while weaving a net of greed [*yoku:* 欲] over the fields, behaving like a long-armed spider, robbing people's sight, a transient wild goose passing through the world; one never again shall possess the heart and mind of one who steals water for "my" rice field. One need not constantly strain to raise

one's voice, reciting the *nembutsu*—such is not needed, for the Buddha deigns to protect us. Hence, the so-called great peace of spirit [*anjin:* 安心]. (6.156-57)

Many Pure Land Buddhists recite the *nembutsu* prayer, "*Namu Amida Butsu*" ("All praise to Amida Buddha!"), as if the words by themselves are a formula that assures their rebirth in the Pure Land. Shinran, however, insists—and Issa a-grees—that salvation has nothing to do with saying a prayer. In his major doctrinal work, *Kyōgyōshinshō* ("True Teaching, Living, Faith, and Realizing of the Pure Land"), Shinran writes that the "mind of Amida" enters the believer's corrupt mind once it has been opened in an atti-tude of faith; it is Amida's mind, not the ego, that enables salvation and so gives rise to *anjin:* a deep and abiding feeling of inner peace (59-60). One can finally relax and stop fretting about en-lightenment because eons ago Amida Buddha, through his causal vow, absolutely assured it.

Following Shinran, Issa scorns those *nem-butsu* chanters who believe that they are in full control of their destinies by merely invoking Amida's name. Such practitioners, Issa argues, have not moved beyond covetousness, for their desire for personal salvation is as insidious and as spiritually damaging as the greed of a farmer who steals water from a neighbor's field. A key phrase in the passage is the "net of greed" that covers the fields, suggesting that one covets all that he or she sees, including, particularly, fields that belong to others. Those who think to save themselves by chanting the *nembutsu* are as avaricious, he claims, as long-armed spiders (*tenaga-gumo:* 手長蜘). In fact, they are thieves, since having "long arms" is a Japanese euphemism for kleptomania. They seek to steal that which can only be freely given: the Buddha's salvation. The Jōdoshinshū Buddhist cannot "earn" rebirth in the Pure Land any more than a Christian, by personal effort, can earn redemption. No one's arms are *that* long! In both religious systems, grace is required. Shallow Buddhism arises from the covetousness of hearts and minds. Such believers attempt to water their own rice fields by stealing from their neighbors. Here Issa uses a variant of the Japanese idiom, *gaden insui* (我田引水): "hauling water to *my* rice field," an expression that denotes the promotion of one's self-interest at another's expense. But to care only about one's own field, one's own future life, runs contrary to Shinran's teaching. Peace of spirit (*anjin*) comes only when one ceases the struggle to win paradise and trusts absolutely in Amida's original vow.

The haiku that follows Issa's discussion of salvation at the end of *Oraga haru* gives poetic expression to this idea of submission to the Buddha.

ともかくもあなた任せのとしの暮
tomokaku mo anata makase no toshi no kure
(616.19)

come what may
trusting in the Buddha . . .
the year ends

As we saw in the Introduction, the eminent scholar, D. T. Suzuki, cites this poem as evidence that Issa was a "worldly" and "spiritually poor" man obsessed with his personal problems (62). His assessment is an unfortunate consequence of the twentieth century's overemphasis on the poet's life, particularly the hardships thereof. However, in the whole context of *Oraga haru*, and coming as it does immediately after Issa's little treatise on Pure Land salvation, this final haiku of the diary conveys a feeling of release from personal anxiety and grateful surrender to Amida Buddha. Although he had every right to complain at the end of a year that saw the death of his precious Sato, Issa's mood at the close of 1819 is one of faithful resignation.

This resignation explains the curious nonchalance that he often manifests in haiku that touch on his own future life rebirth. Of the possible paths of the Six Ways scheme of Buddhist reincarnation, the worst is to return as a sufferer in King Emma's hell. Nevertheless, Issa's tone when mentioning this grim prospect is surprisingly casual.

地獄へは斯う参れとや閑古鳥

jigoku e wa kō maire to ya kankodori

(349.4)

"This way to hell,
pilgrim!"
mountain cuckoo

世の中は地獄の上の花見哉

yo no naka wa jigoku no ue no hana-
mi kana (212.17)

in this world
over hell, viewing
spring blossoms

Issa might be on the road to hell, but what a
lovely road it is, graced by the haunting melody of
the *kankodori*. In the second haiku—which bears
the prescript, "Hell," in Issa's 1812 series on the
Six Ways—the underworld of torment that lurks
beneath the surface of things fails to spoil the
beauty of the blossoms. The poet's unruffled attitude vis-à-vis hell might at first appear impious.
Although Buddhists of Issa's culture considered
rebirth in hell a temporary, not eternal, damna-
tion; it was no picnic. The tenth century monk
Genshin, a widely-read Japanese Dante, describes King Emma's prison with gruesome detail:
"The fire possessed by man is like snow when
compared to this. With the least of physical
contact, the body is broken into pieces the size of
mustard-seeds. Hot iron pours from above like a
heavy rainfall, and in addition, there is a forest of
swords, with blades of exceptional keenness, and
these swords, too, fall like rain" (qtd. in Tsunoda
194).

Issa seems immune to such scare tactics. In
fact, he reports in one of his diaries that he
viewed a pictorial representation of Genshin's
nightmare vision of hell. In 1804 Seventh Month,
16th day, he visited Daijōji, a temple at which he
viewed a painting of hell's Sword District. Two
haiku commemorate the experience.

秋の風剣の山を来る風か

aki no kaze tsurugi no yama wo kuru kaze ka
(467.7)

does the autumn wind
reach the Mountain
of Swords?

秋の風我が参るはどの地獄

aki no kaze waga ga mairu wa dono jigoku
(467.8)

autumn wind—
on my pilgrimage
to whatever Hell

Contemplating the Mountain of Swords, Issa wonders out loud: Does the autumn wind reach even there? In the second haiku, he depicts himself strolling to hell, chilled by the autumn wind. But instead of dreading it, he seems to accept his destination casually. In a later version (1811), he appears just as accepting.

涼しさにぶらぶら地獄巡り哉

suzushisa ni bura-bura jigoku mairi kana
(253.16)

in summer cool
ambling down my road
to hell[49]

Issa's levity in his hell poems reveals not a lack of piety but rather the sort of surrendering faith in Amida's power that Shinran recommends: a leave-all-to-the-Buddha unconcern with what lies ahead on destiny's road. Issa's advice at the end of *Oraga haru* bears repeating: "Though completely adrift on the open sea, one should regard . . . the next life with unconcern; whether one is cast before Buddha—to Hell or to Paradise—it is best to leave it all to 'Thy will,' and simply trust" (6.156). For the Jōdoshinshū Buddhist, sin is inevitable. Even good deeds, if one's intention is to earn salvation through them, are sinful, for they are expressions of the ego's "self power." This is the spiritual context in which Issa cheerfully admits and accepts his own sinfulness. Even the first bath of the new year can be a sin.

> 浴みして旅のしらみを罪始め
>
> *yuami shite tabi no shirami wo tsumi hajime*
> (43.8)

> first bath—
> for my journey's lice
> first sin

And yet, as Kaneko Tohta points out, this fact does not at all detract from the pleasantness of the moment (47).[50] In a similar haiku, the poet "confesses" his laziness.

> 今迄は罰もあたらず昼寝蚊屋
>
> *ima made wa bachi mo atarazu hirune kaya*
> (305.19)

no divine punishment yet—
napping
under the net

The key phrase is the first: *ima made wa*—"yet" or "up to now." Divine retribution may come in time, but for now the poet enjoys a pleasant summer nap. Viewed outside of the context of Jōdo-shinshū belief, this haiku seems blatantly irreligious. However, Issa is actually exhibiting authentic piety as he naps, leaving both punishment and salvation in the capable hands of Amida Buddha.

Returning to the subject of prayer, we see that reliance on the Buddha's Other Power is a liberating derailment of ego control that creates a sense of assurance and peace (*anjin*). The *nembutsu* prayer is not a request to be saved but an expression of gratitude for a favor already bestowed. As such, "prayer" is perhaps an inadequate English equivalent for *nembutsu*. More than a collection of words, it is a way of life, a way of thinking . . . and a way of spiritual liberation. It is as natural as breathing.

なむあみだなむあみだとてこき茶哉
namu amida namu amida tote koki cha kana
(113.13)

"Praise Amida!
Praise Amida!"
picking tea leaves

念仏の口からよばる蛍哉

nembutsu no kuchi kara yobaru hotaru kana
(357.19)

the mouth that
praised Amida Buddha
calling fireflies

蚤噛んで口でなむあみだ仏哉

nomi kanda kuchi de namu amida butsu
kana (378.13)

the mouth that gnawed
a flea, praising
Amida Buddha

蝿一つ打てはなむあみだ仏哉

hae hitotsu utte wa namu amida butsu kana
(373.21)

swatting a fly
and praising Amida
Buddha

In the context of Shinran's doctrine, these and
hundreds of similar haiku in Issa's canon can be
viewed as celebrations of Amida Buddha and his
Other Power amid scenes of everyday life. Prayer
is part of life, whether one is laboring in the field,
calling fireflies, cracking a flea, or swatting a fly.
In the latter two haiku, Buddha is praised in
conjunction with the sin of insect killing. Henderson, writing about the last example, detects sar-

casm and satire: "Issa . . . had no use for the conventional Amidists, many of whom—mostly uneducated ones—had twisted the original doctrine to mean that the simple repetition of the formula 'Namu Amida Butsu' would save them from punishment for any sin, even the great sin of taking life" (126).

While Henderson seems correct when he calls the haiku ironic, it might not be satirical. Midway through the *Oraga haru*, Issa "confesses" that he has been "sowing the seeds of a future life in hell, catching the flies that swarm on [his] lap and condemning, one by one, the mosquitoes that rove over [his] table" (6.148). He adds that he has even broken Buddha's law against drinking alcohol. His two-year-old daughter, he writes, seems in her innocence wrapped in the grace of Amida Buddha, but Issa, a fly killer and sake drinker, apparently is dooming himself to hellfire. Such a confession is tongue-in-cheek, since he plainly states later in the same journal that the avoidance of sin is not the way to the Pure Land but is, in fact, a misguided reliance upon "self-power" that will *certainly* condemn one to rebirth in hell. Despite Henderson's detection of satirical intent, the recitation of the *nembutsu* while killing a fly or flea can be viewed as a genuine exercise of faith, an expression of gratitude that might be paraphrased: "Thank you, Amida, for bringing about my enlightenment despite my inescapable sinfulness!"

Because this sense of cosmic gratitude is so ubiquitous in Issa, the *nembutsu* appears in all sorts of poems depicting all sorts of moods. He praises Amida when cherry blossoms bathe him in their iridescent light.

なむなむと桜明りに寝たりけり
namu namu to sakura akeri ni netari keri
(231.2)

praise Buddha!
sleeping in the light
of cherry blossoms

He praises him while viewing the harvest moon.

年よりや月を見るにもなむあみだ
toshiyori ya tsuki wo miru ni mo namuamida
(455.14)

growing old—
even while moon gazing
praising Buddha!

He praises him in moments of comedy.

なむああと大口明けば薮蚊哉
namu aa to ōkuchi akeba yabu ka kana
(369.23)

mouth open wide
to praise Buddha . . .
a mosquito flies in

He (or some person) praises him in the kitchen while preparing food that strict Buddhists have forbidden.

冬篭り鳥料理にも念仏哉

fuyugomori tori ryōri ni mo nebutsu kana
(697.20)

winter seclusion—
cooking a chicken
praising Buddha

And he praises him all through the dark, lonely
night.

長いぞよ夜が長いぞよなむあみだ
nagai zoyo yo ga nagai zoyo namu amida
(446.5)

long!
the night is long
"Praise Amida . . . "

In Issa's poetic vision, the whole universe
resounds with gratitude for Amida's saving grace.
Hailstones clatter and leaves drift down to the
rhythm of the *nembutsu*.

念仏ぶ拍子付たる霰哉
nembutsu ni hyōshi tsuketaru arare kana
(649.24)

keeping the beat
of the prayer to Buddha . . .
hailstones

念仏に拍子のつきし一葉哉

nembutsu ni hyōshi no tsukishi hito ha kana
(588.14)

keeping the beat
of the prayer to Buddha . . .
one leaf falls

In a sense, every haiku in Issa's canon of over twenty thousand can be viewed as a prayer. Even in verses that do not directly reference the *nembutsu* or praying, one senses the quiet joy and sublime gratitude of one who approaches things of this world with the non-forcing, accepting spirit of Shinran's faith. When Issa opens his hands to catch the falling snow . . .

掌へはらはら雪の降りにけり
tenohira e hara-hara yuki no furi ni keri
(642.1)

to my open palms
snowflakes flitting
down

. . . he does so with reverence. In the moment of poetic and Buddhist insight (there's no difference between the two for Priest Issa), the wonders of Nature enter his consciousness and flow onto paper as precious, sacred gifts. The prevailing mood in Issa's immense poetic collection is not disappointment or sorrow—as many of his biographical critics would have us believe—but rather the joyful gratitude that arises naturally from his Pure Land Buddhist appreciation of grace.

According to Jōdoshinshū Buddhism, the remedy for sinful existence in a fallen age is to accept and trust in the Buddha's transforming grace. Shinran locates the source of corruption in this fallen age in the human mind. In one of his hymns, he asserts, "The nature of the mind is pure from the beginning," but "through delusions and perversions" it acquires "defiled karma" (qtd. in *Shōzōmatsu wasan* 107). The only remedy, then, is to leap aboard Amida Buddha's ship of prayer: "When one, on board the 'prayer-ship' of great compassion, rides out in the broad ocean of illuminating Light, the wind of perfect virtue blows softly over the rolling waves of evil. The darkness of ignorance is then broken through, and one quickly enters the Land of Infinite Light" (*Kyōgyōshinshō*, Tran. Suzuki 62). For Shinran, salvation can be instantaneous because there is nothing in the temporal world that needs to be done to make it happen. It has already been brought about by Amida Buddha's "Other Power"; the important thing is simply to realize it. At the moment of genuine realization, Amida's "prayer-ship" floats the believer, regardless of his or her sins or good actions, over "rolling waves of evil" to enlightenment, which is why Shinran boldly declares that even "criminals of the highest degree, blasphemers of the Right Dharma," and "those who are utterly devoid of any stock of merit" can, in "one thought," leap aboard the boat of salvation (3). The person who relies on the Buddha's saving power realizes the Pure Land in *this* life, remaining in the world of suffering but no longer *of* that world.

To receive Amida's grace, or, rather, to realize that its power has already done all that needs to be done to effectuate one's rebirth in the Pure Land, believers must open their heart-minds, trusting all to Buddha.

ともかくもあなた任せかたつぶり

tomokaku mo anata makase ka katatsuburi
(386.4)

come what may
won't you trust in the Buddha
snail?

みだ頼め蛇もそろそろ穴に入

mida tanome hebi mo soro-soro ana ni iru
(536.8)

trust in Amida Buddha!
snake inching
into its hole

Even snails and snakes should trust in the "Beyond" (*anata*), Issa believes, "come what may." In the snake's case, it is especially vulnerable as it slides slowly into its hole. Issa suggests that it would be a good idea for it to place its trust in Amida Buddha's grace, excellent advice for all sentient beings, according to Pure Land Buddhism—else there is no safety.

Cherry blossoms, blooming and dying, inspire this "simply trust" mantra in countless haiku. Here is a sampling.

ただ頼々とや桜咲

tada tanome tada tanome to ya sakura saku
(225.3)

"Simply trust,
simply trust!"
cherry blossoms in bloom

ただ頼桜ぼたぼたあの通り

tada tanome sakura bota-bota ano tōri
(226.11)

"Simply trust!"
the cherry blossoms
trickling down

西へちるさくらやみだの本願寺

nishi e chiru sakura ya mida no honganji
(233.27)

to the west
cherry blossoms scatter . . .
Hongan Temple

The third example is rife with Pure Land
symbolism. Amida's Paradise lies somewhere in
the mythic west; his vow to rescue sentient
beings, enabling their rebirth in Paradise, is
called *hongan:* 本願) the "original vow." It is
appropriate, then, that the blossoms at Honganji,
a temple named after Amida's salvational vow,
scatter toward the west, trusting, as does the
poet, in the Buddha of the west. The sight of
dewdrops dissolving in an autumn field inspires
the same thought.

只頼め頼めと露のこぼれけり

tada tanome tanome to tsuyu no kobore keri

(478.8)

"Simply trust! trust!"
dewdrops spilling
down

And a butterfly in the autumn wind, its stay in
the world almost over, has no recourse but to
place its devout trust in the great "Beyond."

秋風にあなた任の小蝶哉

aki kaze ni anata makase no ko chō kana

(467.13)

in autumn wind
trusting in the Buddha . . .
butterfly

Even mosquitoes find safe harbor in Amida Buddha.

旦の蚊の弥陀のうしろにかくれけり

asa no ka no mida no ushiro ni kakure keri

(370.24)

morning's mosquitoes—
behind Amida Buddha
they hide

We have already seen that Issa ends his *Oraga
haru*, and the year 1819, submitting to the
Buddha.

ともかくもあなた任せのとしの暮
tomokaku mo anata makase no toshi no kure
(616.19)

come what may
trusting in the Buddha . . .
the year ends

It should not surprise us, then, that he begins the
next year, 1820, on the same note.

弥陀仏をたのみに明て今朝の春
mida butsu wo tanomi ni akete kesa no haru
(27.4)

in Amida Buddha
trusting . . .
spring begins

Throughout his life and poetry, Issa is consistent
on this point. Since one cannot earn passage to
the Pure Land through self power, the only
answer is to rely on the Other Power of Amida
Buddha, a power which transforms the individual
and the universe or, more exactly, the individual/
universe in their inseparableness. When one
abandons the fiction of duality, a fiction which
proposes the identification with an ego-self as a
separate entity from the rest of the universe; one
enters the Pure Land instantaneously, escaping
the hopelessness and corruption of the world of
mappō. From that point on, he or she no longer
views things with a rapacious urge to control
them. Instead, the universe and all consciousness
(no difference between the two) are embraced in

the same spirit of surrender and trust made possible by Amida Buddha's Other Power. Issa's haiku can be viewed—correctly, I think—as the records of myriad trusting and accepting encounters of self with universe in which the two disclose their essential unity. When the poet stares at a frog, he is staring at himself . . . staring back.

おれとして白眼くらする蛙かな
ore to shite niramekura suru kawazu kana
(162.11)

locked in a staring contest
me . . .
and a frog

In the Introduction we began with this haiku, noticing how it creates humor through the incongruity of its human and amphibian contestants. However, the congruity in the scene is just as important. Issa and the frog are not only fellow travelers on the road to enlightenment; they are essentially the *same* traveler. To put it another way, "Issa" and "frog" are constructs that exist in separateness only within the either-or framework of human linguistic thinking. To an enlightened perspective—a perspective that transcends either-or thinking and can therefore be talked about only in the language of poetic image and metaphor—there is just one traveler, one struggling point of consciousness, one "I" on a journey to ultimate realization: a journey to a place that has been called, metaphorically, the Pure Land, made possible by a guiding and enabling power that has been called Amida.

NOTES

1. All haiku in this book are taken from Volume 1 of the nine-volume *Issa zenshū*. The number in parentheses refers to the page; the number after the decimal point indicates its position on the page. The present haiku, accordingly, is the eleventh poem on page 162.

2. Traditional Japanese dynastic years ended several weeks after New Year's Day on the Western calendar, usually around mid-February. Issa died on the19th day of Eleventh Month, late enough in the 10th year of Bunsei (1827) to have an actual Western death date of early 1828. Nevertheless, most English commentators list his dates as 1763-1827.

3. In the first edition I used the word "syllabet" to denote a Japanese sound unit. Robin D. Gill coined the word "syllabet" to denote "uniformly short syllables that can be written with a single letter of a phonetic syllabary"—quoted from his manuscript, *Rise, Ye Sea-Slugs!* Though, as it does here, *kana* usually closes a haiku, it is considered a "cutting word" (*kireji*)—one of a group of special particles, most of which divide a verse into two main structural parts of 5/12 or 12/5 syllabets.

4. Issa produced two manuscripts of *Hachiban nikki*. This haiku appears in both, though in slightly different versions. In the first version, the "middle seven" phrase is *kagamikura suru*, which denotes "squatting low to look at" the frog; see *Issa zenshū* 4.37, note 3.

5. Here and henceforth, English translations of Japanese prose are my own unless otherwise designated.

6. In *Shichiban nikki*, 1818, Issa calls himself "Priest Issa" (*Issa-bō*).

春立や弥太郎改め一茶坊

haru tatsu ya yatarō aratame issa-bō (31.9)

new spring—
Yatarō dies, priest Issa
is born

A year later, in a revision of this haiku in *Hachiban nikki*, he ends it, "Haiku Temple" (*hai-kai-ji*).

春立や弥太郎改めはいかい寺

haru tatsu ya yatarō aratame haikai-ji (31.9)

new spring
Yatarō is reborn
into Haiku Temple

7. See Murata Shōcho's 1969 study, *Haikai-ji Issa no geijutsu*, and Kaneko Tohta, *Issa kushū*, 248.

8. 616.19. Perhaps citing from memory, Suzuki misquotes the "top-five" phrase, but this doesn't affect the meaning. Whether Issa begins with *tomokaku mo* or *nanigoto mo*, the idea is one of resignation: "Ah well, in any event . . . ".

9. See Alfred Bloom, *Shinran's Gospel of Pure Grace*, 43-44.

10. See my book, *Issa, Cup-of-Tea Poems; Selected Haiku of Kobayashi Issa* (1991), and my essays, "In Defense of Bad Buddhism . . . and Issa" (1996), "At the Crossroads of Six Ways: A Haiku Buddhist Vision of Life, Death, and Everything" (1996), "Issa and Buddhism" (2001), and (published after the first edition of this book) "The Haiku Mind: Pure Land Buddhism and Issa" (2008).

11. Despite the prevailing opinion of the Japanese critics, Sam Hamill removes the ambiguity of the prescript in his translation, rendering it as if Issa definitely wrote the haiku at age six: "[W]hen only six years old, I wrote . . ." (50).

12. Shinji Ōgawa notes that Issa, who lost his haiku master (Chikua) the previous year, was determined to set off on a walking tour to claim

his destiny as a haiku master. Shinji writes, "The last line, 'it's a world of the beggar with the plum blossoms' may mean, 'It's my world now!'"

13. Takashi Kasegawa, president of the Shiki Museum in Matsuyama, kindly explained this poem and the comical situation that it portrays when I visited there.

14. There is yet another possible meaning to this haiku. The kanji for "ocean" (*umi:* 海) contains within it the Japanese character, "mother" (*haha:* 母). Perhaps Issa is reminded of his mother every time he sees or writes the word "ocean," since "mother" is part of it.

15. At the time of this haiku's composition, First Month 1820, Issa was living on his side of the divided house with his wife, Kiku. Two of their children had already died: Sentarō in 1816 and Sato in 1819.

16. Another example of misassigned biographical connection concerns this haiku, which Henderson claims refers to the death of one of Issa's children (123).

> 露ちるやむさい此世に用なしと
>
> *tsuyu chiru ya musai kono yo ni yō nashi to*
> (477.21)
>
> dewdrops scatter—
> "Goodbye, cruel
> world!"

This haiku was composed in 1813, a year before his marriage and three years before the arrival of his and Kiku's firstborn, Sentarō.

17. I am indebted to Hiroshi Kobori for helping me to understand this haiku. Hiroshi notes that Issa uses the word *no* ("field") instead of *ta* ("rice field") because the mention of *nae* ("rice stalk") already indicates that it is a rice paddy. To use both *ta* and *nae* in in the haiku would be, in his opinion, "too much."

18. Compare this to Robert G. Henricks' translation: "The highest humanity takes action, yet it has no reason for acting this way" (98). A biblical analogue to this concept is Jesus's admonition that one should keep one's deeds of mercy secret (Matt. 6.4).

19. Issa writes dozens of haiku about the 1819 eclipse in his journal, *Hachiban nikki*. In *Oraga haru*, he reprises four of them, including one of the ones quoted here ("world of man—/ even the moon/ suffers!"; 6.154). The French translator, Coyaud, presents this haiku without mentioning the eclipse. Without this information, what are his readers to make of the statement, "the moon, too/ is sick" ("*La lune elle aussi/ A des maladies*" 85)?

20. Shinji Ogawa has helped to untangle the syntax of Issa's original. *Ku no shaba ya:* "painful (or afflicting) world . . . "; *sakura ga sakeba:* "if cherry blossoms bloom"; *saita tote:* "because of the blooming." He paraphrases:

painful world . . .
if cherry blossoms bloom
because of the blooming (the blooming adds
another pain)

He comments, "We Japanese smile at Issa's twist to associate the blooming of cherry blossoms with pain." R. H. Blyth's two translations of this haiku are less accusatory of the blossoms: it is "A world of grief and pain" but "Even then" the blossoms bloom; or, in his second version, it is such a world "Even when" they have bloomed, not *because* they have done so (*Haiku* 1.168; 2.614). Munier's French translation follows Blyth: it's a world of pain " . . . alors meme que les cerisiers/ sont en fleur" (25).

21. For example:

人足のほこりを浴るさくら哉
hito ashi no hokori wo abiru sakura kana
(234.11)

bathed in the dust
of people's feet . . .
cherry blossoms

22. *Hikaraji* and *magaraji* in these two haiku are negative forms of the verbs, *hikaru* (to shine) and *magaru* (to be crooked). See Blyth, *History* 1.384.

23. Although Hamill cites the story as if it really took place (xxi), as does the French trans-

lator Collet, who quotes it in its entirety (14-17); contemporary critics in Japan regard it as a fabrication. It is hard to imagine gentle Issa lashing out against "traitors" (*zoku*) to haiku art. And, as Shinji Ōgawa observes, Issa was an inveterate note-taker who turned practically everything that happened to him into haiku. If he had actually met Lord of Kaga under such unusual circumstances, he would have certainly written about it.

24. A related haiku composed at the time has a prescript in which Issa writes that he was stricken with paralysis on the previous Tenth Month, 16th day, and nearly died. Now, however, he greets the new year "as a reborn person walking the earth." Shinji Ōgawa adds, "This haiku expresses his joy of recovery from paralysis. He expresses his joy with the down-to-earth word 'profit.'" Though the term *shaba* has Buddhist connotations, suggesting the notion of the Latter Days of Dharma, Shinji believes that Issa is using the word to mean "this world," without religious connotations.

25. Shinji Ōgawa believes that the phrase, "wanting nothing in this world," can be interpreted in two ways: (1) satisfaction with this world; or (2) a feeling of hopelessness about this world. He thinks that Issa is saying the latter. I believe that Issa's haiku implies a third possibility: the butterfly flaunts and celebrates its detachment from the hopeless world.

26. Shinji Ōgawa notes that *hokekyō* (Lotus

Sutra) onomatopoetically echoes the sound of a nightingale's warble.

27. Kai Falkman observes that the phrase *no kage*, which denotes "in the shadow of," has a secondary meaning of "protected by" or "thanks to" (54). In light of this double meaning, an alternative translation might read,

> thanks to cherry blossoms
> no one
> is a stranger.

28. An earlier version of this chapter was published in essay form; see my essay, "Transience in Issa."

29. The language parodies the famous battle cry of Chinzei Hachirō Tametomo, a twelfth century warrior and strongman. More on this in Chapter 6.

30. Lewis Mackenzie prints a different ending to this haiku not found in *Issa zenshū*: *moto no mizu* ("Throw it back in the water!"; 45). This seems to be an error.

31. For example, Titus-Carmel in 1994 (99), Hass in 1994 (196), and Hamill in 1997 (170) published versions of the "tub-to-tub" poem without advising readers that it might be apocryphal. As recently as 2012, Stephen Addiss includes the "snow-on-the-quilt" haiku as Issa's work in his book, *The Art of Haiku: Its History*

through Poems and Paintings by Japanese Masters.

32. Some of the material in this chapter appeared first in my talk, "Issa and Buddhism," which I delivered at the Global Haiku Festival at Millikin University in Decatur, Illinois, April 2000. The text of this talk was published subsequently in *Modern Haiku*.

33. Or, as Susumu Takiguchi argues, *several* frogs plopped into Bashō's famous pond. He writes, "Who decided that this haiku talked about only a single frog? . . . It is not our usual experience to see a single frog in early spring in Japan, which is the time when this haiku was composed. Also, the sound of water is not normally a single plop, or splash. More importantly, the haiku depicts a cheerful and merry scene whereby frogs are noisy, and there's life everywhere . . . far from the standard interpretation of a world of tranquility and eternal stillness" (25).

34. Shinji Ōgawa alerted me to the fact that Issa's first and second phrases in this haiku echo a well-known, pre-Tang Dynasty Chinese poem by Tao Qian (also known as Tao Yuanming). His poem, "I Built My House Near Where Others Dwell," has the lines: "I pluck chrysanthemums under the eastern hedge,/ And gaze afar towards the southern mountains" (66). Shinji writes, "The

two lines depict a very serene and refined tone, and then Issa introduces a frog in the third line. The contrast makes the haiku very humorous."

35. Shinji Ōgawa writes, "Commonly, there is a pine tree around the entrance of the traditional Japanese house. The pine tree is normally well-trimmed. I think Issa's 'wild pine' means an untrimmed pine." If this is true, the unkempt pine serves as a metaphor for the poet—just as his "trashy house" (*kuzuya*) does in other poems. In Pure Land Buddhist terms, Issa embodies the ideal of non-striving naturalness, being "just as I am." Furthermore, if one views this haiku as an allusion to the New Year's custom of decorating one's gate with pine and bamboo, Issa's point seems clear and consistent with many similar statements in his poetry and prose: the wildly growing pine will suffice to decorate his gate; he will do nothing but trust in Nature's spontaneity.

36. Although some poets today spurn invention and insist upon capturing an authentic, present "haiku moment" (Tasker 50-53), Issa was adept at both methods, sometimes recording the scenes before him and at other times creating them from a deep place in his heart and mind.

37. A decade later, in *A History of Haiku*, Blyth retranslates: "No talents,/ And so no sin . . . " (392), a rendering that appears to have influenced Collet's French version: "sans mérite/ sans péché" (167). Yuasa translates the opening of the haiku differently: "An old duffer, if you like,/ But yet no criminal" (132), utterly eliminating the poem's Buddhist flavor. Hamill's first lines stray

even farther from Issa's original text: "Suspicious character/ maybe, but no crook" (90).

38. In the first poem, Issa's verb (*chidori*) describes the action of measuring out a lot on which to build a house. The second poem also makes use of an old expression: *kumiai suru*, meaning to wrestle; see Nakada 1049; 520.

39. This seems more appropriate than prissy English euphemisms, such as Blyth's "Commit no nuisance" (*History of Haiku* 1.376) or Stryk's "Be respectful" (58). The French translator, Collet, seems to agree with me, rendering Issa's warning to the sparrows, *défense de pisser* ("no pissing allowed!" 80).

40. Some English translators soften Issa's bluntness. Yuasa has the old woman merely wipe her nose with the petals of the flower, not mentioning the nasal discharge (64). Hamill uses the same delicate phrasing (27).

41. Titus-Carmel, in her French translation, assumes that *tashō no en* refers to another soul's karma: "*karma d'une autre ame*" (32). Blyth, more reasonably, believes that Issa is marveling at how he and the butterfly must have been connected in a previous lifetime: "This also is the Karma of a previous life" (*Haiku* 2.553).

42. Another haiku with a butterfly/karma connection is the following.

蝶の身も業の秤にかかる哉

chō no mi mo gō no hakari ni kakaru kana
(171.9)

the butterfly too
on the scales of karma
is weighed

43. Japanese critics also tend to overlook the Buddhism inherent in Issa's treatment of animals. Yoshida, for example, devotes a chapter of a book to the topic of Issa and animals ("Horses' Issa, Sparrows' Issa": 馬の一茶、雀の一茶) without mentioning Buddhism or reincarnation (139-68).

44. Literally, Issa is saying that he wishes to be reborn as a meadow butterfly. The word, *mutsumaji*, translated here as "sweet harmony," denotes a sense of gentle friendliness. Shinji Ōgawa believes that Issa is specifically referring to a male and female couple. The poet uses this same expression to describe gentle, tame deer in a temple town, most likely Nara.

足枕手枕鹿のむつまじや
ashi makura temakura shika no mutsumaji ya (521.21)

my feet for a pillow
and my hands . . .
the friendly deer

45. The last two examples involve a katydid (*kirigirisu*), a green or light brown insect that is a cousin of crickets and grasshoppers. The males

possess special organs on the wings with which they produce shrill calls. Although katydid is the closest English translation, Blyth uses the more familiar "cricket" in his translation of the first haiku, of which he translates a variant form found in *Issa hokku shū* (1. 549); see *Haiku* 4.1070. In Blyth's English version of the second haiku, he switches gears and calls the same insect a grasshopper (*Haiku* 4.1068).

46. In his translation, Stryk has the cats worshipping "the God of Love" (38), a substitution that radically changes the haiku's meaning.

47. In *Issa, Cup-of-Tea Poems*, I translated Kompira as "the sea-god" (79), but I now believe, in this context, Kompira functions more in his capacity as guardian of travelers.

48. The opening phrase, *kero-kero*, is a form of *kerorikan*, a word that Issa coined, denoting "the appearance of showing no concern or interest" (Nakada 574).

49. The editors of *Issa zenshū* suggest another dimension to this haiku: "Hell" might possibly be a pseudonym for a prostitute whom Issa is on his way to visit (3.121).

50. Shinji Ōgawa explains that Issa is punning in this haiku. The final phrase, *tsumi hajime*, not only denotes first "sin" (*tsumi*), it suggests that the poet has begun "pinching" the lice, after his bath (*tsumu* = to pinch).

WORKS CITED

Addiss, Stephen. *The Art of Haiku: Its History through Poems and Paintings by Japanese Masters*. Boston & London: Shambhala, 2012.

Bashō. *The Narrow Road to the Deep North and Other Travel Sketches*. Tran. Nobuyuki Yuasa. New York: Penguin, 1966; rpt. 1981.

Bloom, Alfred. *The Life of Shinran Shonin: The Journey to Self-Acceptance*. Leiden: E. J. Brill, 1968.

-----. *Shinran's Gospel of Pure Grace*. Tucson: U. of Arizona Press, 1956.

Blyth, R. H. *Haiku*. Tokyo: Hokuseido, 1949-1952; rpt. 1981-1982 [reset paperback edition]. 4 vols.

-----. *A History of Haiku*. Tokyo: Hokuseido, 1964; rpt. 1969. 2 vols.

Carter, Steven D. *Traditional Japanese Poetry: An Anthology*. Stanford, Calif.: Stanford Univ. Press, 1991.

Cheng, Man-jan. *Lao-Tzu: "My words are very easy to understand"*. Tran. Tam C. Gibbs. Richmond, Calif.: North Atlantic Books, 1981.

Cholley, Jean. *En village de miséreux: Choix de poèmes de Kobayashi Issa.* Paris: Gallimard, 1996.

Cohen, William H. *To Walk in Seasons: An Introduction to Haiku.* Rutland, Vermont & Tokyo: Charles E. Tuttle, 1972.

Collet, Hervé and Cheng Wing Fun. *Issa: et pourtant, et pourtant.* Millemont: Moundarren, 1991.

Coyaud, Maurice. *Tanka, haiku, renga: le triangle magique.* Paris: Société d'édition Les Belles Lettres, 1996.

Dobbins, James C. "From Inspiration to Institution: The Rise of Sectarian Identity in Jōdo Shinshū." *Monumenta Nipponica* 41, 3 (1986): 331-43.

Dykstra, Yoshiko Kurata. "Jizō, the Most Merciful. Tales from Jizō *Bosatsu Reigenki.*" *Monumenta Nipponica* 33, 2 (1978): 179-200.

Falkman, Kai. *Understanding Haiku: A Pyramid of Meaning.* Winchester, VA: Red Moon Press, 2002.

Fujimoto Jitsuya 藤本實也. *Issa no kenkyū* 『一茶の研究』. Tokyo: Meiwa Insatsu, 1949.

Hall, John Whitney. *The Cambridge History of Japan.* Vol. 4: Early Modern Age. Cambridge: Cambridge University Press, 1991; rpt. 1994.

Hamill, Sam. *The Spring of My Life and Selected Haiku by Kobayashi Issa*. Boston & London: Shambhala, 1997.

Harada Tasuku. "Japanese Character and Christianity: A Study of Japanese Ethical Ideals as Compared With Teachings of Christianity." *Pacific Affairs* 2, 11 (Nov. 1929): 693-98.

Hass, Robert. *The Essential Haiku: Versions of Basho, Buson,and Issa*. Hopewell, New Jersey: Ecco Press, 1994.

Henderson, Harold G. *An Introduction to Haiku*. New York: Doubleday, 1958.

Henricks, Robert G. *Lao-Tzu: Te-Tao Ching*. New York: Ballentine, 1989.

Higginson, William J. with Penny Harter. *The Haiku Handbook: How to Write, Share, and Teach Haiku*. New York and Tokyo: Kodansha, 1985; rpt. 1989.

Huey, Robert N. "Journal of My Father's Last Days: Issa's *Chichi no Shūen Nikki*." *Monumenta Nipponica* 39,1 (1984): 25-54.

Hurvitz, Leon, trans. *Scripture of the Lotus Blossom of the Fine Dharma*. New York: Columbia U. Press, 1976.

Jaffe, Richard M. *Neither Monk Nor Layman: Clerical Marriage in Modern Japanese*

Buddhism. Princeton & Oxford: Princeton University Press, 2001.

Jones, Bob. "Seasonality." *Modern Haiku* 27, No. 3 (1996): 47-50.

Kaneko Tohta. 金子兜太. *Issa kushū* 『一茶句集』. Tokyo: Iwanami Shoten, 1983; rpt. 1984.

Keene, Donald. *Anthology of Japanese Literature from the earliest era to the mid-nineteenth century*. New York: Grove, 1955.

Kenkō. *Essays in Idleness*. Tran. Donald Keene. New York: Columbia U. Press, 1983.

Kobayashi Issa 小林一茶. *Issa zenshū* 『一茶全集』. Ed. Kobayashi Keiichirō [小林計一郎]. Nagano: Shinano Mainichi Shimbunsha, 1976-1979. 9 vols.

Kobayashi Keiichirō 小林計一郎. *Kobayashi Issa* 『小林一茶』. Tokyo: Kissen Kōbunkan, 1961.

Kobayashi Takeshi. *Nara Buddhist Art: Todai-ji*. Tran. Richard L. Gage. New York & Tokyo: Weatherhill/Heibonsha, 1975.

Kurata Hyakuzo. *Shinran*. Tran. Umeyo Hirano. Tokyo: Cultural Interchange Institute for Buddhists, 1964.

Kuriyama Riichi 栗山理一. *Kobayashi Issa* 『小林一茶』. Tokyo: Chikuma Shobō, 1970; rpt. 1974.

LaFleur, William R. *The Karma of Words: Buddhism and the Literary Arts in Medieval Japan.* Berkeley: U. of California Press, 1983.

Lanoue, David G. "At the Crossroads of Six Ways: A Haiku Buddhist Vision of Life, Death, and Everything." *Modern Haiku* 27, No. 3 (1996): 60-70.

-----. "The Frog Poems of Issa: A Look at Nine Haiku." *Modern Haiku* 16, No. 1 (1985): 17-25.

-----. "The Haiku Mind: Pure Land Buddhism and Issa." *Eastern Buddhist* 39.2 (2008): 159-76.

-----. "In Defense of Bad Buddhism . . . and Issa." *Modern Haiku* 27, No. 2 (1996): 56-66.

-----. "Issa and Buddhism." *Modern Haiku* 32, No. 1 (2001): 35-40.

-----. *Issa, Cup-of-Tea Poems; Selected Haiku of Kobayashi Issa.* Berkeley: Asian Humanities Press, 1991.

-----. "Transience in Issa." *Modern Haiku* 32, no. 2 (2001): 37-45.

-----. "Translating Translations: A Disturbing Trend." *Modern Haiku* 31, No. 2 (Summer 2000): 53-58."

Levy, Ian Hideo. *The Ten Thousand Leaves: A Translation of the Man'yōshū.* Vol. 1. Princeton, N.J.: Princeton U. Press, 1981.

Mackenzie, Lewis. *The Autumn Wind: A Selection from the Poems of Issa.* London: John Murray, 1957; rpt. Tokyo: Kodansha International, 1984.

Maruyama Kazuhiko 丸山一彦. *Issa haiku shū* 『一茶俳句集』. Tokyo: Iwanami Shoten, 1990; rpt. 1993.

Miner, Earl, et. al. *The Princeton Companion to Classical Japanese Literature.* Princeton: Princeton University Press, 1984.

Miyamori Asatarō. *Haiku Poems, Ancient and Modern.* Tokyo: Maruzen, 1932; rpt. 1940.

Mōri Hisashi. *Sculpture of the Kamakura Period.* Tran. Katherine Eickmann. New York & Tokyo: Weatherhill/Heibonsha, 1974.

Munier, Roger. *Haïku.* Paris: Librairie Arthème Fayard, 1978.

Murasaki Shikibu. *The Tale of Genji.* Tran. Arthur Waley. New York: Doubleday, 1955.

Murata Shōcho 村田昇著. *Haikai-ji Issa no geijutsu* 『俳諧寺一茶の藝術』. Shimonoseki: Genshashin, 1969.

Nakamura Rikurō 中村六郎. *Issa senshū* 『一茶選集』. Kyoto: Kyoto Insatsusha, 1921; rpt. 1930.

Nakada Shūmi 中田祝未, Ed. *Kogo daijiten* 『古語大辞典』. Tokyo: Shogakukan, 1983.

Nouet, Noel. *The Shogun's City: A History of Tokyo*. Tran. John & Michele Mills. Sandgate, Folkstone England: Paul Norbury, 1990.

Nihon kokugo daijiten 『日本国語大辞典』. Tokyo: Shogakukan, 1972-76. 20 vols.

Ôshiki Zuike 黄色瑞華. *Jinsei no hiai: Kobayashi Issa* 『人生の悲哀小林一茶』. Tokyo: Shintensha, 1984.

Ross, Nancy Wilson. *Buddhism: A Way of Life and Thought*. New York: Vintage Books, 1981.

Shinran. *The* Kyōgyōshinshō: *The Collection of Passages Expounding the True Teaching, Living, Faith, and Realizing of the Pure Land*. Tran. D. T. Suzuki. Kyoto: Shinshu Otaniha, 1973.

-----. *The Letters of Shinran*. Tran. Yoshifumi Ueda. Kyoto: Hongwanji International Center, 1978.

-----. *Shōzomatsu wasan: Shinran's Hymns on the Last Age*. Kyoto: Ryukoku U. Press, 1980.

Stryk, Lucien. *The Dumpling Field: Haiku of Issa*. Athens Ohio: Swallow Press, 1991.

Suzuki, D. T. *Shin Buddhism*. New York: Harper & Row, 1970.

Takiguchi Susumu. "Japan Has Embarked on Her Voyage to World Haiku." *Proceedings of The 1st International Contemporary Haiku Symposium*. Tokyo: Gendai Haiku Kyōkai, 1999. 23-25.

Tao Qian. *T'ao the Hermit, Sixty Poems by T'ao Chi'en (365-427)*. Trans. William Acker. London & New York: Thames and Hudson, 1952.

Tasker, Brian. "In Defence of the Haiku Moment—A Response to Haruo Shirane." *Modern Haiku* 31, No. 2 (2000): 50-53.

Titus-Carmel, Joan. *Issa: Haiku*. Vendome: Éditions Verdier, 1994.

Tsunoda Ryusaku, et. al. *Sources of Japanese Tradition*. Vol. 1. New York: Columbia U. Press, 1958; rpt. 1964.

Virgil, Anita. "Issa: The Uses of Adversity." *Snow on the Water: The Red Moon Anthology of English-Language Haiku*. Winchester, Virginia: Red Moon Press, 1998: 128-46.

Whitman, Walt. *Complete Poetry and Selected Prose*. Ed. James E. Miller. Boston: Houghton Mifflin, 1959.

Yoshida Miwako 吉田美和子. *Issa burai* 『一茶無頼』. Nagano: Shinano Mainichi Shimbunsha, 1996.

Yuasa Nobuyuki. *The Year of My Life: A Translation of Issa's* Oraga Haru. Berkeley: U. of California Press, 1960; 2nd ed. 1972.

ABOUT THE AUTHOR

David G. Lanoue is a professor of English at Xavier University of Louisiana. He is a cofounder of the New Orleans Haiku Society, an associate member of the Haiku Foundation, and former president of the Haiku Society of America. His books include translations (*Issa's Best: A Translator's Selection of Master Haiku* and *Cup-of-Tea Poems: Selected Haiku of Kobayashi Issa*), criticism (*Pure Land Haiku: The Art of Priest Issa* and *Issa and the Meaning of Animals: A Buddhist Poet's Perspective*), and a series of "haiku novels": *Haiku Guy, Laughing Buddha, Haiku Wars, Frog Poet,* and *Dewdrop World.* Some of his books have appeared in French, German, Spanish, Bulgarian, Serbian, and Japanese editions. He maintains *The Haiku of Kobayashi Issa* website, for which he translated 10,000 of Issa's haiku.

34357287R00128

Made in the USA
Middletown, DE
20 August 2016